WHAT IS
SPIRITISM?

WHAT IS
SPIRITISM?

INTRODUCTION TO KNOWING THE INVISIBLE WORLD, THAT IS, THE WORLD OF SPIRITS

Containing

THE FUNDAMENTALS OF THE SPIRITIST DOCTRINE AND A RESPONSE TO SOME OF THE MAIN OBJECTIONS AGAINST IT

by

Allan Kardec

Allan Kardec

AUTHOR OF *THE SPIRITS' BOOK* AND OF *THE MEDIUMS' BOOK*

Without Charity there is no Salvation

Translated by Darrel W. Kimble, Marcia M. Saiz and Ily Reis

Copyright © 2010 by
INTERNATIONAL SPIRITIST COUNCIL
SGAN Q. 909 – Conjunto F
70790-090 – Brasilia (DF) – Brazil

ISBN 978-85-7945-026-6

Original French Title:
QU'EST-CE QUE LE SPIRITISME ?
(Paris, 1859)

Translated by Darrel W. Kimble, Marcia M. Saiz and Ily Reis

Cover design by: Luciano Carneiro Holanda
Layout: Rones José Silvano de Lima

Edition of
INTERNATIONAL SPIRITIST COUNCIL
SGAN Q. 909 - Conjunto F
70790-090 - Brasilia (DF) - Brazil
www.edicei.com
edicei@edicei.com
55 61 3038 8400
Sales: + 55 61 3038 8425

Authorized edition by International Spiritist Council

Second Edition 10/2011

INTERNATIONAL DATA FOR CATALOGING IN PUBLICATION (ICP)

K27g   Kardec, Allan, 1804-1869.

What is Spiritism? : introduction to knowing the invisible world, that is, the world of spirits / by Allan Kardec; [translated by Darrel W. Kimble, Marcia M. Saiz and Ily Reis]. – Brasilia, DF (Brazil): International Spiritist Council, 2011.
220 p.; 21 cm

Translated from: Qu'est-ce que le spiritisme ?

ISBN 978-85-7945-026-6

1. Spiritism. I. International Spiritist Council. II. Title.

CDD: 133.9
CDU: 133.7

Contents

CHAPTER II

CHAPTER III

BIOGRAPHY OF ALLAN KARDEC[1]

Ladies and Gentlemen,

Many persons who are interested in Spiritism often express the regret of having only a very imperfect understanding of the biography of Allan Kardec, and of not knowing where to find information regarding the one whom we call Master. Therefore, it is to honor Allan Kardec and celebrate his memory that we find ourselves gathered here today, since one and the same sentiment of veneration and recognition stirs all our hearts with regards to the Founder of the Spiritist philosophy. In an attempt to respond to such a legitimate desire, please allow me to talk to you for a few moments about that beloved Master, whose works are universally known and appreciated, and whose inner life and industrious existence may only be imagined.

If it were easy for all the conscientious investigators to acknowledge the great significance and scope of Allan Kardec's work by carefully reading his productions, then due to the absence even today of means for doing so, very few could enter the private life of the man and follow him step by step in the performance of his task, so grand,

---

[1] In keeping with the Portuguese version published by the Brazilian Spiritist Federation, and translated by Guillon Ribeiro, we have included this short biography of Allan Kardec by Henri Sausse. It is an abridgement of a lengthier version (available in French at www.spiritisme.net/ouvrages/kardec.htm) and was read by the author at a gathering of Spiritists in Lyon for the March 31, 1896 observance of the 27th anniversary of Kardec's passing. – Tr.

so glorious and so well-accomplished. Not only is Kardec's biography little-known, it has yet to be written at all. Envy and jealousy have sown the most obvious errors, the grossest and most impudent slander about it. Therefore, I shall make every effort to show you, in the truest light, the Great Initiator, whose disciples we are proud to be.

You all know that our city can be honored aright for having witnessed within its walls the birth of that fearless and methodical thinker, that wise, clear-sighted and profound philosopher, that tireless worker, whose labor shook the religious edifice of the Old World and established the new foundations that would serve as the basis for the evolution and renewal of our decaying society, impelling it toward a saner and loftier ideal, toward intellectual advancement and sound morals.

It was in Lyon, on October 3, 1804 that a child was born into an old Lyon family by the name of Rivail - he, who would later bear the illustrious name of Allan Kardec, and who would earn so much acclaim and our deepest affection and recognition.

In this regard, here is a positive and official document: "October 12 of the year XIII[2], birth certificate of *Denizard Hippolyte-Leon Rivail.* Yesterday at 7:00 p.m., the son of *Jean-Baptiste Antoine Rivail,* magistrate and judge, and *Jeannne Duhamel,* his wife, residents of Lyon, 76 Sala Street[3] was born. The child's sex was recognized as male. Major witnesses: *"Syriaque-Frederic Dittmar,* director of the mineral water establishment on Sala Street, and *Jean-François Targe* of the same Sala Street, at the request of the physician, *Pierre Radamel,* 78 Saint-Dominique Street. After reading it, the witnesses signed it, as did the Mayor of the South Zone."

President of the Court,

(Signed): Mathiou

---

[2]   1813 – Tr.

[3]   The house in which Allan Kardec was born disappeared during the enlargement and reconstruction of Sala Street from 1840 to 1852, following the floods of 1840.

At birth, the future founder of Spiritism received a dear and respected name, and an entire past of virtue, honor and probity. Due to their talent, knowledge and scrupulous probity, many of his forebears had distinguished themselves in law and magistracy. One might think that the young Rivail would also have dreamed of being granted the honor and glory of his family in the same capacity. Such was not to be, however, because from the beginning of his youth he felt attracted to the sciences and philosophy.

Rivail Denizard did his initial studies in Lyon, and then completed his schooling in Yverdun (Switzerland) with the famous professor Pestalozzi, of whom he would soon become one of the most eminent disciples, as well as an intelligent and dedicated collaborator. He applied himself wholeheartedly to spreading the educational system that exerted such a great influence on the reformation of education in France and Germany.

Quite often, when Pestalozzi was called away here and there by governments to found institutes similar to the one in Yverdun, he entrusted Denizard Rivail with the job of replacing him in the management of his school. His disciple-turned-master had, above all and with the most legitimate right, the ability required to handle the job that had been entrusted to him. He received his bachelor's in letters and sciences, and then a doctorate in medicine after having completed all his medical studies and having brilliantly defended his dissertation. A renowned linguist, he had in-depth knowledge of and was fluent in German and English. He also knew Dutch and could easily express himself in that language. Denizard Rivail was a tall, handsome young man with distinct manners. He was kind and obliging, and in private he displayed jovial good humor. When it was time for his mandatory military service, he obtained an exemption and two years later went to Paris to found an establishment at 35

Sevres Street similar to that of Yverdun. For this undertaking, he associated himself with one of his uncles, his mother's brother, to be his financier.

In Paris, Denizard Rivail frequented the world of letters and teaching, and in doing so he met Miss Amelie Boudet, a teacher. She was petite but well proportioned, kind and gracious, well-off (due to her parents), an only child, intelligent and lively. Her smile and character led her to be noticed by Mr. Rivail. And under this affable man's frank and communicative cheerfulness, she perceived the learned and profound thinker who combined great dignity and propriety. The civil records inform us that: "Amelie-Gabrielle Boudet, daughter of Julien-Luis Boudet, proprietor and notary public, and Julie-Louise Seigneat de Lacombe, was born in Thiais (Seine) on November 23, 1795." Miss Boudet was thus nine years older than Mr. Rivail, but she looked ten years younger. On February 6, 1832, the marriage contract was signed in Paris on Sevres Street by Hippolyte-Leon-Denizard Rivail, director of the Technical Institute (Pestalozzi Method), son of Jean-Baptiste Antoine and Mrs. Jeanne Duhamel, residents of Chateau-du-Loir, and Amelie-Gabrielle Boudet, daughter of Julien-Louis and Mrs. Julie-Louise Seigneat de Lacombe, residents of 35 Sevres Street in Paris.

Rivail's partner had a passion for gambling and he ruined his nephew by losing huge sums at Spa and at Aix-la-Chapelle. Rivail petitioned for the liquidation of the Institute, and each was given his share of 45,000 francs. This amount was entrusted by Mr. and Mrs. Rivail to one of their close friends, a businessman, who was involved in bad business. He went bankrupt and left nothing to his creditors. Far from becoming discouraged by this double setback, Rivail courageously threw himself into his work. He managed to do the accounting for three places, which provided him with around 7,000 francs per year. In the evening, when his day was finished, this tireless worker wrote books on grammar and arithmetic, in addition to volumes on higher pedagogical studies. He translated works from English and German, and prepared all the courses for Levy-Alvares, which was frequented by both sexes from the suburb of *Saint-Germain*. Furthermore, in his home on Sevres Street, he organized free courses in chemistry, physics, astronomy and comparative anatomy, which were highly attended from 1835 to 1840. He was a member of several learned societies – most notably the Royal Academy of Arras – and in 1831 he was awarded for the presentation of his noteworthy essay: *What system of education is most in harmony with the needs of the time?*

Among his numerous works, the following are cited in chronological order: *Plan proposé pour l'amélioration de l'instruction publique* (Plan Proposed for the Improvement of Public Education), 1828; in 1829 according to the Pestalozzi method, he published for use by teachers and wives *Cours pratique et théorique d'arithmétique* (Practical and Theoretical Course on Arithmetic); in 1831 he published *Grammaire française classique* (Classical French Grammar); in 1846 *Manuel des examens pour les brevets de capacité* (Examination Manual for receiving the Aptitude Diploma), which entailed rational solutions to questions and problems in arithmetic and geometry; in 1848 he published *Catéchisme grammatical de la langue française* (Grammatical Catechism of the French Language); finally, in 1849 we find Mr. Rivail teaching at Lycée Polymathique, filling chairs in physiology, astronomy, chemistry and physics. In a highly significant work, he summed up his courses and later published: *Dictées normales de examens de l'Hôtel de Ville et de la Sorbonne* (Standard Dictations for the examination of the Hotel de Ville and the Sorbonne) and *Dictées spéciales sur les difficultés orthographiques* (Special Dictations on Orthographic Difficulties). These various works were adopted by the University of France and were sold profusely; thus, Rivail managed a modest income, thanks to them and his tireless work.

As one may tell from this very brief exposition, Denizard Rivail was wonderfully prepared for the hard task he would have to perform and render successful. His name was recognized and respected, and his works justly appreciated long before he immortalized the name Allan Kardec.

Pursuing his teaching career, Rivail was able to live happily, honorably and peacefully, having rebuilt his fortune through persevering work and the brilliant success that crowned his efforts. However, his mission would call him to a more onerous task, to a greater work, and as we will many times demonstrate, he always showed that he was capable of the glorious mission that had been reserved for him. His natural propensities and aspirations might have led him to mysticism, but his education, correct judgment and methodical observation kept him sheltered from nonsensical enthusiasm and unjustified negations. It was in 1854 that Mr. Rivail first heard about "turning tables" from the magnetizer Mr. Fortier, with whom he maintained a relationship due to their studies on magnetism. Mr. Fortier said to him one day, "There is something quite extraordinary about this; not only is the table made to turn by magnetization, but it is also made to communicate. If it is asked something, it responds." "That," retorted Mr. Rivail, "is another matter. I will believe it when I see it and when it has been proven to me that a table has a brain for thinking, nerves for feeling and that it can become a somnambulist. Until then, allow me to regard it as nothing more than a fairytale to make me feel sleepy."

Such was Rivail's state of mind in the beginning, and thus we will see him many times, not denying something *parti pris*, but asking for proof and wanting to see and observe in order to believe. Such must be our conduct regarding a subject as attractive as manifestations from the Beyond. Up to this point, we have only been concerned with talking about Mr. Rivail, professor emeritus, pedagogical author of renown. However, from 1854 to 1856, a new horizon was opening to this profound thinker, this astute observer. During that time of his life, the name of Rivail was overshadowed to give way to that of Allan Kardec, whose fame would be taken to all corners of the globe, which every echo would repeat, and which all our hearts would treasure.

Here is how Kardec revealed his doubts, his hesitations and also his first initiation: "Thus, I found myself faced with an inexplicable fact that seemed contrary to the laws of nature and which my reason rejected. I still had not seen or observed anything; the experiments done in the presence of honorable and worthy individuals of faith did convince me that a purely physical effect was possible, but the idea of a *talking* table still had not even entered my mind. The following year – toward the beginning of 1855 – I met Mr. Carlotti, a friend for twenty-five years, who talked about these phenomena for more than an hour with the same enthusiasm he put into all new ideas. Mr. Carlotti was Corsican by birth and possessed of an ardent and energetic nature. I had always perceived in him the qualities that characterize a great and beautiful soul, but I distrusted his enthusiasm. He was the first to speak to me about the intervention of spirits, but he only added to my doubts. "Someday, you will be one of us," he said. "I will not say no," I responded. "We shall see."

"Some time later, during May of 1855, I was in the home of the somnambulist Mrs. Roger with Mr. Fortier, her magnetizer. There, I met Mr. Patier and Mrs. Plainemaison, who spoke to me about the phenomena just as Mr. Carlotti had, but in a different tone. Mr. Patier was a civil servant of certain age, a highly educated man with a serious, cool and composed nature. His deliberate speech was devoid of any enthusiasm and made a lively impression on me; and when he invited me to witness some experiments that would be performed in Mrs. Plainemaison's home on 18 Grange-

Bateliere, I readily accepted. The engagement was set for the next Tuesday[4] at 8:00 p.m. It was there that for the first time I witnessed the phenomenon of the turning tables, which jumped and moved about in such a way that doubting the matter was not possible.

"I also saw a few very imperfect attempts at mediumistic writing on a slate with the help of a basket. I was far from changing my mind, but there had to be some sort of cause behind such an incident nonetheless. Behind those apparent futilities and the type of game that the phenomena were used for, I glimpsed something more serious, perhaps revealing of a new law, and I promised myself I would delve into it. The opportunity presented itself and I was able to observe the phenomenon more closely than I had been able to before. During one of Mrs. Plainemaison's soirees, I made the acquaintance of the Baudin family, who lived on Rochechouart Street at the time. Mr. Baudin invited me to witness some weekly sessions at his home, which I attended diligently from that time onward. It was there that I made my first serious studies in Spiritism, still less due to the revelations than to the observations. I applied the experimental method to this new science as I had always done before then; I never formulated preconceived theories; I observed closely, comparing and deducing the consequences; I sought to go back to the causes from the effects through deduction, through the logical chain of facts, and did not accept an explanation as valid unless it could resolve all the difficulties of the issue. That is how I had always proceeded with my previous endeavors since I was fifteen or sixteen years old. From the very start, I grasped the gravity of the exploration I was going to undertake. I saw in these phenomena the key to the very obscure and controversial problem of humanity's past and future, the solution that I had sought for my entire life. It was, in a word, a complete revolution

---

4   The date was left blank in the manuscript. – Pub.

in my ideas and beliefs; hence, I had to act circumspectly and not lightly; I had to be positivistic and not idealistic to keep from allowing myself to become deluded.

"One of the first results of my observations was that spirits, being nothing more than human souls, were endowed with neither supreme knowledge nor supreme wisdom, that their knowledge was limited to the degree of their evolution, and that their opinions had value only as personal opinions. I recognized this truth at the start, and it enabled me to avoid the grave mistake of believing that spirits were infallible, and it also kept me from formulating premature theories based on the opinion of only one or a few of them. The mere fact that one could engage in communication with spirits – no matter what they might say – proved the existence of an unseen world surrounding us. This was a crucial point, an immense field ripe for exploration, the key to a multitude of inexplicable phenomena. The second, no-less important point was in understanding the state of that world and its customs – if I may so express myself. I soon observed that, due to its personal position and knowledge, each spirit disclosed an aspect of that world precisely as one would come to understand the state of a country by questioning the inhabitants of all classes and conditions. Each one would be able to teach us something, but none of them by themselves would be able to teach us everything. It would the observer's responsibility to formulate the whole with the help of documents gathered from different places and collected, coordinated and compared with one another. Thus, I acted with the spirits as I would with persons: for me, they were, from the least to the highest, a means of gathering information and not *predestined revelators*."

To this information, which is contained in Kardec's *Posthumous Works*, we must add that, from the start, Mr. Rivail – far from being enthusiastic about those manifestations and absorbed by his other concerns – was at the point of abandoning them. He might have actually done so if not for the pressing solicitations of Mr. Carlotti, Mr. Rene Taillandier (member of the Science Academy), Mr. Tiedeman-Manthese, the Sardous (father and son) and Mr. Didier (publisher), who for five years had followed the study of the phenomena and had gathered *fifty notebooks containing many communications*, which they had not been able to put in order. Since they knew about Rivail's immense and rare aptitude for synthesizing, these gentlemen gave him the notebooks, asking him to take cognizance of them and to put them in order. This task would be arduous and would require much time due to the gaps and obscurities in the communications, so the learned encyclopedist turned down such a tiresome and time-consuming task due to his other responsibilities.

One night, his protector spirit, Z, through a medium, gave him an altogether personal communication, in which it stated, among other things, that it had known him in a previous existence, when, at the time of the Druids, they had lived together in Gall. At that time he was called Allan Kardec, and since they had been such great friends, this spirit had promised to help him in the highly important task to which he had been called, and which he would readily see through to the end. Consequently, Mr. Rivail threw himself into the work. He took the notebooks and carefully annotated them. After a close reading, he eliminated the repetitions and put each dictation and each session report in its proper order. He highlighted the gaps to fill, the obscurities to clarify, and prepared the questions needed to achieve this result.

"Until then," said Mr. Rivail, "the sessions in Mr. Baudin's home had no definite purpose. I therefore proposed to resolve the problems that interested me from the viewpoints of philosophy, psychology and the nature of the invisible world. I came to each session with a series of prepared questions that were methodically proposed. They were responded to with precision, depth and logic. From that time on, the meetings took on a much different character, and among the observers there were serious individuals who took a lively interest in the work. If I happened to miss, the sessions became erratic, since the majority was not interested in futile questions. In the beginning, I had only my own instruction in mind; later, when I saw that everything was forming a whole and was taking on the proportions of a doctrine, I got the idea to publish the work for widespread instruction. These were the same questions, successively developed and completed, which comprised the foundation for *The Spirits' Book*."

In 1856 Mr. Rivail often attended Spiritist meetings held on Tiquetonne Street in the home of Mr. Roustan with Miss Japhet, who was a somnambulist and who as a medium received highly interesting communications with the help of a beaked basket. Through this medium, Mr. Rivail examined the communications that were received and put in order beforehand. This work took place at first during ordinary sessions, but at the Spirits' request, and so that more care could be dedicated to them and more attention given to examining them, it was continued during private sessions. "I was not happy with such verification the Spirits had recommended to me," says Allan Kardec. "Having been placed by the circumstances in rapport with other mediums, every time the occasion arose, I took advantage of it to propose a few questions that seemed thorny. It was thus that more than ten mediums cooperated in that work. And it was from the comparison and joining of all these responses, which were coordinated, classified and many times reorganized in the silence of meditation, that I formed the first edition of *The Spirits' Book*, which appeared on April 18, 1857."

This book was in large format with two columns per page: one for the questions and the other for the responses. At the time it was published, the author was quite puzzled at how to sign it: as Denizard-Hippolyte-Leon Rivail or under a pseudonym. Since his name was very well-known in the scientific world due to his previous works, which could cause confusion and even harm the success of the undertaking, he adopted the latter and signed it using the name Allan Kardec, which, according to what his Guide had revealed, was what he had been called during the time of the Druids. The work achieved such success that the first edition was soon sold out. Kardec re-edited it in 1858[5] under the current format. It was reviewed, corrected and expanded considerably.

On March 25, 1856, Allan Kardec was in his office in order to consult the communications and prepare *The Spirits' Book*, when he heard repeated raps in the walls. He tried but failed to discover their cause and then went back to work. His wife came in at around 10:00 a.m. and heard the same noises. They both looked but failed to determine the source. At the time, Mr. and Mrs. Kardec lived at 8 Martyrs St. in the back of the second floor. Kardec wrote, "Since the following day there were sessions at Mr. Baudin's home, I told him what had happened and asked if he could explain it."

Question: *You have heard the incident that I have just mentioned. Could you tell me what caused the raps, which so insistently made themselves heard?*

Answer: It was your familiar spirit.

Question: *What was his purpose for knocking in this way?*

Answer: He wanted to communicate with you.

Question: *Can you tell me what he wanted?*

Answer: You can ask him yourself; he is right here.

Question: *My familiar spirit, whoever you may be, I thank you for having visited me. Would you be so kind as to tell me who you are?*

Answer: For you I shall call myself *Truth*, and for a quarter of an hour every month, I will be here at your disposal."

---

[5] The second edition appeared in April 1860, the third in August 1860, the forth in February 1861 – three editions in less than one year - auth.

Question: *Yesterday, when you rapped while I was working, did you have something in particular to tell me?*

Answer: I wanted to tell you about the work you were doing. What you were writing was disagreeable to me and I wanted to make you stop."

REMARK: What I was writing was related precisely to the studies I was making concerning spirits and their manifestations.

Question: *Did you disapprove of the chapter I was writing or the work as a whole?*

Answer: About yesterday's chapter: you be the judge; re-read it this evening. You will recognize your errors and you will correct them."

Question: *Actually, I myself was not very satisfied with that chapter and I have already reworked it. Isn't it better now?*

Answer: It is better, but still not very good. Read the third to the thirtieth line and you will find a serious error."

Question: *I tore up what I did yesterday!*

Answer: The tearing does not prevent the error from remaining. Re-read it and you will see."

Question: *Is the name* Truth, *which you have taken, an allusion to the truth I am seeking?*

Answer: Perhaps; at least it is a guide that will protect and help you."

Question: *May I evoke you in my home?*

Answer: Yes, so that I may assist you through thought. But as for written responses in you home, it is too soon for you to be able to receive them."

Question: *Could you come more often than once per month?*

Answer: Yes, but I can only promise once per month until further notice."

Question: *Have you indwelled some personage known on earth?*

Answer: I have told you that for you I am Truth; this name for you means discretion. You do not need to know more than that."

Upon returning home, Allan Kardec rushed to re-read what he had written and found the serious error that he had committed. The one-month interval set for each communication from the Spirit *Truth* was rarely observed. He manifested frequently to Kardec, but not at his home, where for almost a whole year he was unable to receive communications through any medium; every time he hoped to receive one, he was prevented by some unforeseen cause opposing it.

It was on April 30, 1856 in the home of Mr. Roustan and through the medium Miss Japhet that Allan Kardec received the first revelation about the Mission he was to fulfill. Such notice was rather vague at first, but was clarified on June 12, 1856 by the medium Miss Aline C. On May 6, 1857, Mrs. Cardone, by inspecting Kardec's hand lines[6] confirmed the two previous communications, which she did not know about. Finally, on April 12, 1860, in Mr. Dehan's home and through the medium Mr. Crozet, that mission was once again confirmed in a spontaneous communication obtained in Kardec's absence. The same applied regarding his pseudonym. Several communications in different places reaffirmed and corroborated the first communication regarding it. Urged on by events and documentation he had in his possession, and due to the success of *The Spirits' Book*, Kardec came up with a plan to create a Spiritist journal. He approached Mr. Tiedeman to ask for his financial support, but the latter decided not to take part in this undertaking. On November 15, 1857, through the mediumship of Miss E. Dufaux, Kardec asked

---

[6] "I had the opportunity to meet Mrs. Cardonne during Mr. Roustan's sessions. Someone told me – I think it was Mr. Carlotti – that she had the remarkable talent of reading palms. I had never believed that the lines on the palm had any meaning whatsoever, but I had always thought that, for certain persons gifted with a sort of second sight, it could be a way to establish a relationship that enabled them, just like somnambulists, to say things that were sometimes true. In such a case, the signs of the palm would be nothing more than a pretext, a way to focus the attention, to develop lucidity, similar to cards, coffee grounds and so-called magic mirrors for other persons who enjoy the faculty of second sight. The experiment once again confirmed the correctness of that opinion." (Allan Kardec, *Posthumous Works*, pt. 2, *"The Spiritual Tiara"*) – Tr.

his Guides what he should do. He was told to carry out his idea and not worry about anything.

He stated, "I hurried to write the first issue, which appeared on January 1, 1858, without my having told anyone. I did not have even one subscriber or financial partner. Thus, I published it entirely at my own risk. I did not regret it, because its success surpassed my expectations. From January 1 onward, the issues were published without interruption, and as the Spirit had foreseen, the journal became a powerful aid for me. I realized later that I was lucky not to have found a financial partner because I enjoyed more freedom, whereas an interested outsider would have intended to impose his ideas and will on me and could have hindered my progress. By myself, I did not have to answer to anybody no matter how onerous the work was."

This duty continued to increase in the amount of work and responsibility, and involved constant struggles against obstacles, attacks and perils of all sorts. Nonetheless, to the degree that the work became more intense and the struggle more acute, this energetic worker rose to the challenge, a fact that never came as a surprise. For eleven years, via *Revue Spirite* (which, as we have just seen, had started out so modestly), he confronted all storms, all competitions, and was spared no jealousy, as he himself affirmed, and as he had been forewarned about when his mission was revealed. That communication and Kardec's thoughts show us in an unflattering light the situation at the time, but they also highlight the great worth of Spiritism's founder and his merit for having known how to overcome it all.

Medium, Miss Aline C., June 12, 1856:

Question: What are the causes that can make me fail? The insufficiency of my aptitudes?

Answer: No. But missions of reformers are full of obstacles and dangers; yours is difficult – let me warn you – for it involves the stirring up and transformation of the whole world. Do not think it will be enough to publish one book, two books, ten books, while remaining undisturbed in your home. No, you must get involved in the conflict. Terrible hatred will be aroused against you; implacable enemies will plot your ruin; you will be exposed to slander and betrayal, even from those who seem to be most devoted to you; your best teachings will be attacked and twisted; you will succumb more than once to the weight of fatigue; in other words, you will have to bear an almost constant struggle, sacrificing your rest, your peace, your health and even your life, for you will not live very long. So then, more than one missionary retreats when, instead of a flowered pathway, he finds his steps lined only with thorns, sharp stones and serpents. For such missions, intelligence is not enough. Before anything else, to please God, one needs humility, modesty and unselfishness, for he strikes the proud and presumptuous. In order to struggle against the human element, one must have courage, perseverance and unshakable firmness. One must also be prudent and tactful in order to deal with things appropriately and not to compromise their success with untimely measures and words. Finally, one must be devoted, self-denying and ready for any kind of sacrifice. You can see that your mission will depend on the conditions that you yourself set."

The spirit *Truth*

COMMENT (by Kardec): I am writing this on January 1, 1867, ten and a half years after that communication was given to me, and I can affirm that everything has happened as it said at every point, for I have experienced all the vicissitudes predicted by it. I have been the target of the hatred of implacable enemies, of insult, slander, envy and jealousy. Infamous libels have been published against me; my best teachings have been twisted. I have been betrayed by those in whom I had placed my trust and have been paid with ingratitude by those to whom I rendered service. The

Parisian Society has been a continual focus of intrigue conspired by those who said they were on my side, and who, pretending to be amiable in my presence, stabbed me in the back. It has been said that those who adopted my position were bribed by me with money that I collected from Spiritism. I have not known what rest is; more than once I succumbed due to excessive work; my health has changed and my life compromised. Nevertheless, thanks to the protection and assistance from the good Spirits, who have ceaselessly given me manifest proofs of their solicitude, I am happy to realize that I have not experienced one single instant of breakdown or discouragement, and that I have unswervingly pursued my duty with the same ardor, without worrying about the evil of which I was the target. According to the Spirit *Truth's* communication, I was to expect all this and everything has occurred.

* * *

When we read about all his struggles, all the turpitudes of which Allan Kardec was the target, how elevated he becomes in our sight and how his brilliant triumph acquires merit and splendor! What became of those envious persons, those little minds who sought to prevent his progress? Most of their names are unknown or no longer awaken any remembrance. Oblivion has overtaken them and has forever buried them in darkness, whereas Allan Kardec, the intrepid combatant, the daring pioneer, will pass on to posterity with his halo of glory so rightly won.

The Parisian Society for Spiritist Studies was founded on April 1, 1858. Until then, meetings had been held in Kardec's home on Matyrs Street, with Miss. E. Dufaux as the main medium. The room started out with fifteen to twenty people, but soon there were more than thirty. Thus, this location became overcrowded, and not wanting to burden Kardec with all the duties, a few assistants proposed forming a Spiritist society and rented another place for holding the meetings. However, in order to meet, they had to obtain the recognition and authorization of the Police. Mr. Dufaux, who knew the Chief of Police personally, was in charge of taking the necessary measures, and thanks to the Interior Minister, General X., who was favorable toward new ideas, the authorization was obtained in only fifteen days, whereas if the normal route had been taken, it would have required months with no guarantee of success. The Society was then legally formed and meetings were held every Tuesday in the place that had been rented in the Palais-Royal, Valois Mall. Meetings continued to be held there for one year, from April 1, 1858 to April 1, 1859. When it could remain there no longer, the society gathered every Friday in one of the rooms at the Douix Restaurant in the Palais-Royal Montpensier Mall from April 1, 1859 to April 1, 1860, at which time the Society moved into its own headquarters on 59 Sainte-Anne. After having given account of the conditions in which the Society was formed and the task he had to fulfill, Kardec explained *(Revue Spírite*, 1859, p. 169):

"In pursuit of my duties, which I must say were quite laborious, I used all the diligence and dedication of which I was capable. From the administrative point of view, I worked to maintain strict order at the meetings and to impress them with a serious character, without which the assembly's reputation would have soon vanished. Now that my job is over and the impulse has been provided, I should inform you of my decision to renounce in the future any kind of position in the Society – even that of director of its studies. I do not aspire to any titles except that of a simple charter member, with which I will always feel happy and honored. My reason for this is in the multiplicity of my tasks, which increase everyday through the extension of my relationships, because besides those you know about, I am preparing other, more considerable projects, which require long and laborious study and which will demand no less than ten years. In addition, the duties of the Society will not cease to take a lot of time, whether in preparing or coordinating and putting everything in order. They require assiduity, which often interferes with my personal duties, thus rendering my almost exclusive initiative indispensable in the tasks assigned to me. That is the reason, gentlemen, of which I had so often spoken, frequently deploring the fact that our eminently enlightened members have deprived us of their light. For a long time, I have nurtured the desire to resign my duties: I have expressed it very explicitly on several occasions, whether here or in private with my colleagues, especially with Mr. Ledoyen. I would have done it much earlier if I had not feared causing a disturbance in the Society. If I had resigned in the middle of the year, it might have been regarded as desertion, and I could not give such pleasure to our adversaries. Therefore, I saw my duties through to the end; now, however, those reasons no longer apply, and I have hurried to tell you about my decision in order not to hinder the choice you will make. It is only right that all have their share in the duties and honors."

We must hasten to add that Kardec's resignation was not accepted and he was reelected unanimously except for one blank vote. In the light of this affirmation of affinity, he gave in and retained his duties.

In September of 1860, Kardec took a promotional trip to our area, and it was then that reference was made to the Parisian Society for Spiritist Studies:

"Mr. Allan Kardec has given a report on the results of his recent trip in the interests of Spiritism, and is happy about the cordial welcome he received everywhere, especially in Sens, Macon, Lyon and Saint-Etienne. Wherever he stayed, he observed the Doctrine's remarkable progress; however, what is especially worthy of note is that nowhere did he see it being used as entertainment; on the contrary, everywhere it was taken very seriously; everywhere its scope and consequences for the future were understood. Of course, there are many adversaries, of whom the most obstinate are the self-interested, but scoffers have decreased considerably; seeing that their sarcasm does not put the mockers on their side, and that they help more than hinder the progress of the new beliefs, they have begun to understand that they gain nothing with their behavior and that it is a waste of energy; hence, they keep quiet. One highly characteristic phrase seems to be the order of the day everywhere, which is: *"Spiritism is in the air"*; that by itself depicts the current state of affairs. The most noteworthy results occurred in Lyon, where there are numerous Spiritists of all social classes, and the blue-collar class is composed of hundreds. The Spiritist Doctrine has had the healthiest influence on the laborers from the point of view of order, morality and religious ideas. In sum, the spread of Spiritism continues with the most heartening speed."

Following his trip, Kardec made a magisterial speech at a banquet held on September 19, 1860. We will quote a few passages appropriate for our purposes, we who worthily aspire to replace these workers of the first hour:

"The first thing that impressed me was the number of followers. I knew perfectly well that Lyon had a huge number, but I was far from imagining that there were so many. There are hundreds, and in a short time – I hope – we will not be able to count them.

"However, if Lyon stands out because of its numbers, it does no less so in terms of quality, which is even worthier. Nowhere did I encounter anything but sincere Spiritists, who understood the Doctrine from its true point of view. There are three categories of followers, gentlemen. First, there are those who limit themselves to believing in the reality of the manifestations and who before anything else seek out the phenomena; for them, Spiritism is simply a series of more or less interesting phenomena. Second, there are those who see something in Spiritism besides the phenomena, who understand its philosophical scope and admire the morality that derives from it; however, they do not put Spiritism into practice. For them Christian charity is a pretty maxim, but nothing more. Third, there are those who are not content with simply admiring its morality; they practice it and accept its consequences. They are well convinced that earthly existence is a passing trial, and they make every effort to take advantage of these short moments to progress on the path of evolution that the Spirits have traced out for them by doing their utmost to do good and to restrain their evil tendencies. Being in a relationship with them is always safe because their convictions keep them from every thought of evil. *On every occasion, charity is the rule of their conduct.* These are *true Spiritists*, or better, *Christian Spiritists*.

"Well then, gentlemen, I am happy to tell you that in Lyon I did not find one follower from the first category; nowhere did I see Spiritism regarded as a mere curiosity or with frivolous motives. Everywhere, the purposes and intentions were serious, and believing what I was told, there are several from the third category. Therefore, we must pay homage to the Lyon Spiritists for having generously entered upon the evolutionary path, without which Spiritism would have no purpose! Their example will not be futile; it will have its consequences. And it was no wonder that the Spirits responded to me the other day through one of your most devoted mediums, albeit the least known, when I expressed my surprise, *'Why do you marvel at it? Lyon has always been a city of martyrs; faith is alive there; it shall furnish apostles for Spiritism. If Paris is the head, Lyon will be the heart.'*" Kardec's opinion concerning the Lyon Spiritists of his time is a great honor for us, but it must also be a rule of conduct. All Spiritists in their turn must make every effort to deserve such praise, by taking our master's lessons to heart, and, especially, conforming their behavior to them. *Noblesse oblige*, states an adage. Let us all remember this and keep Spiritism's banner flying high and firmly. However, Kardec was not content with simply throwing flowers at our co-workers. More than that, he provided them with wise counsels, upon which we must in turn meditate.

"Since the teaching comes from the Spirits, the various groups, as well as individuals, find themselves under the influence of certain spirits who preside over their work, or who guide them morally. If these spirits are not found to be in agreement, the issue is to know which one deserves the greatest trust. It will obviously be the one whose theory does not provoke any serious objection; in other words, the one who at every point provides the greatest proof of being of a high order. If everything it teaches is good and rational, it matters little what name the spirit has assumed. In this regard, the matter of identity is entirely secondary. If, under a respectable name, the teaching fails in its essential qualities, we may immediately conclude that it is an apocryphal name and that it is an impostor or frivolous spirit. *General Rule: the name is never a guarantee*; the *sole true guarantee that it is a high order spirit is its thought and the way it expresses itself.* Any deceiving spirit can imitate anything except true wisdom and true sentiment.

"It oftentimes happens that, in order to make individuals adopt various utopias, some spirits exhibit a false wisdom and think they can impose it by choosing from their arsenal of technical words anything that might delude the gullible. And they have an even surer method: they put on the appearance of virtue, and with the aid of great words such as charity, fraternity and humility they hope to promulgate the grossest absurdities; and that is exactly what happens whenever we are not on our guard. Hence, we must avoid allowing ourselves to be seduced by appearances both on the part of spirits and human beings. I must confess that that is one of the greatest difficulties, but I have never said that Spiritism is an easy science. It has its stumbling blocks that can only be avoided through experience. In order to avoid this trap, we must above all run from blind enthusiasm and from the pride that leads certain mediums to believe themselves to be the sole interpreters of the truth. *Everything must be coolly examined, maturely weighed and tested.* And if we distrust our own judgment – which is often quite prudent to do – we must resort to other persons according to the proverb, 'Four eyes are better than two.' Only false self-love or an obsession could make a notoriously wrong idea persist, one which anyone's common sense would reject." Those are the wise and practical counsels given by the one who others wanted to be taken as an enthusiast, a mystic or a visionary, and this rule of conduct, established from the start, has not yet proven invalid either by observation or by the phenomena themselves. It has always been the safest and wisest route, the only one that should be followed by those who want to concern themselves with Spiritism.

At that time, Kardec was working on *The Mediums' Book*, which appeared during the first two weeks of January, 1861, published by Mr. Didier & Cia., Booksellers and Publishers. The master explains its reason for being in *Revue Spirite* in the following terms: "We sought in this work – the fruit of much experience and hard study – to clarify all the issues attached to the practice of spirit manifestations. According to the Spirits, it contains the theoretical explanation for the various phenomena and the conditions in which they may be produced. However, the part dealing with the development and practice of mediumship was especially the object of full, special attention on our part. *Experimental Spiritism is surrounded with many more difficulties than is generally believed, and the obstacles that may be encountered are numerous.* This is what produces so much deception on the part of those who concern themselves with it without having the necessary experience or understanding. Our aim was to caution investigators against such pitfalls, which are not always exempt from inconveniences for whomever might want to imprudently venture forth into this new realm. We could not ignore such a crucial point, and we treated it with care equal to its importance."

The Mediums' Book is still the handbook for all who want to delve into the practice of experimental Spiritism. Nothing better or more complete has yet appeared on the subject. It is still the surest guide for us to be able to safely explore the realm of mediumship.

* * *

In 1861, Allan Kardec took another Spiritist trip to Sens, Macon and Lyon, and saw that Spiritism in our city had reached its maturity.

"Actually, I did not count just hundreds of Spiritists as I had done a year before. I counted thousands; rather, I could hardly determine their numbers, and I calculate that if things progress as they have, then within a year or two there will be more than thirty thousand. In Lyon, Spiritism has acquired followers from all social classes, but it is especially in the blue-collar class that it has spread most quickly. This is nothing to marvel at: the working class is the one that suffers most and it will turn to the side that offers it the greatest consolation. If those who rail against Spiritism were to offer workers from this class as much, they would look to them. But on the contrary, our opponents want to take away precisely what would help such people bear their burden of misery. But this approach has been the surest way to lose their sympathy and to cause them to swell our ranks. What we have seen with our own eyes is so characteristic and contains such a great teaching that we believe we should devote most of our report to these workers. Last year there was only one meeting center, that of the Brotteaux's, headed by the shop foreman Dijoux and his wife. Thereafter, other centers were organized in different parts of the city: Guillotiere, Perrache, Croix-Rousse, Vaise, Saint-Just, etc., not including a large number of private meetings. Previously, there were only two or three neophyte mediums; today, there are mediums at all the centers and many are of the highest quality. In one group alone we saw five writing at the same time. We also saw a young man who was a seeing medium and we can attest to the fact that this faculty was developed to the highest degree. Of course, we highly desire for the number of followers to grow, but what is more valuable than quantity is quality. Now let us emphatically state: nowhere did we see Spiritist meetings that were more edifying than those of the Lyon working class regarding order, concentration and attention paid to the instructions of their spirit guides. There were men, seniors, women, young people, even children, whose respectful attitude contrasted with their age. Not once did a single child for one moment disturb the silence during our often-drawn out meetings. They seemed almost as enthusiastic as their parents in hearing what we had to say. But that is not all: the number of moral metamorphoses among the working class is almost as large as the number of followers: nasty habits reformed, passions subdues, hatreds pacified, homes turned peaceful; in other words, the most authentic Christian virtues had developed; all because of their unshakable trust in spirit communications, and in the future that they had not believed in previously. It is a joy for them to receive these communications, from which they derive comfort in the face of adversity. Many of them come from more than three miles away in any kind of weather – winter or summer – braving everything in order not to miss a session. Theirs is not an ordinary faith, but one based on a profound, rational conviction that is in no way blind."

On account of this trip, the members of the large Lyon Spiritist family were gathered again under Kardec's presidency for another banquet. On September 19, 1860, there had been only 30 guests in attendance; on September 19, 1861, there were 160, "representing the various groups, who all regarded themselves as members of one big family, and among whom there was not a shadow of jealousy or rivalry, which, (said the master) incidentally, we have the great satisfaction to report. Most of those in attendance were blue-collar workers and everyone noticed the perfect order that reigned at every moment. That was so because true Spiritists are satisfied with joys of the heart and not those of noisy pleasures."

On October 14 of the same year, we find Allan Kardec in Bordeaux, where, as in all the cities through which he passed, he sowed the Good News and caused faith in the future to germinate.

Besides Kardec's trips and duties, the year 1861 will remain memorable in the annals of Spiritism for an incident that was so monstrous as to seem almost beyond belief. I am referring to the book burning in Barcelona that resulted in three hundred Spiritist books being burned by the fire of inquisitors. Mr. Maurice Lachatre was at that time the bookseller in Barcelona. As he had a relationship with Kardec and agreed with his ideas, he asked Kardec to send him a certain number of Spiritist books so that he could sell them and advertise the new philosophy. Approximately three hundred books were shipped under ordinary conditions, with a packing slip attached to the boxes. When they arrived in Spain, the customs fees were charged to the addressee and collected by agents of the Spanish government. However, the boxes were not delivered. The Bishop of Barcelona judged the books to be pernicious to the Catholic faith, and had the shipment confiscated by the Holy Office. Since the church did not want to deliver the books to the addressee, Kardec asked for them to be returned; however, his request was ignored and the Bishop, who, raising himself to the status of an enforcer in France, based his refusal on the following response: "The Catholic Church is universal, and since these books are contrary to the Catholic faith, the government cannot consent to allowing them to pervert the morality and religion of other countries."

Not only were the books not returned, but the Spanish treasury kept the customs duties. Kardec could have pursued a diplomatic action to obligate the Spanish government to return the books. The Spirits, however, dissuaded him, saying that it was preferable for the spread of Spiritism to let all this ignominy follow its course.

Reenacting the history and fires of the medieval era, the Bishop of Barcelona had the incriminated books burned in the public square at the hand of the executioner. Following is a passage from the historical document containing the statements of the infamous cleric:

"On October 9, 1861, at 10:30 a.m., in the public square of the city of Barcelona, in the area in which criminals condemned to the ultimate punishment are executed, and by order of the Bishop of this city, three hundred books and brochures concerning Spiritism were burned, to wit:

"*Revue Spirite*" [Spiritist Review][7], edited by Allan Kardec;

"*Revue Spiritualiste*" [*Spiritualist Review*] edited by Pierart;

"*Le Livre des Esprits*" (*The Spirits' Book)* by Allan Kardec;

"*Le Livre des Médiums*" (*The Mediums' Book)*, by Allan Kardec;

"*Qu'est-ce que le Spiritisme?*" (*What is Spiritism?)* by Allan Kardec;

"*Fragment de Sonate*" *[Sonata Fragment]*, dictated by Mozart's spirit;

"*Lettre d'un catholique sur le Spiritisme*" *[Letter by a Catholic concerning Spiritism]*" by Doctor Grand;

"*L'Histoire de Jeanne d'Arc*"*[The Story of Joan of Arc]*, dictated by her to Miss Ermance Dufaux;

"*La Réalité des Esprits Démontrée par l'Écriture Directe*" *[The Reality of Spirits Demonstrated by Direct Writing]*, by the Baron of Guldenstubbe.

Witnesses to the book burning:

"A priest dressed in sacramental attire holding a cross in one hand and a torch in the other;

---

[7] Titles in brackets are the works which have *not yet* been translated into English by the International Spiritist Council – Tr.

"A notary public in charge of drawing up the verbal proceedings for the book burning;

"The notary public's scrivener;

"A top-level customs administrator;

"Three *mozos* (servants) of the customs office in charge of stoking the fire;

"A customs agent representing the owner of the books condemned by the Bishop;

"An incalculable crowd gathered on the promenade and covered the forecourt on which the fire burned.

"After the fire had consumed the three hundred Spiritist volumes and brochures, the priest and his assistants withdrew in the midst of jeers and curses from many observers, who were shouting: 'Down with the Inquisition!' Next, several persons approached the fire to gather up the ashes."

It would be diminishing the horror of this act if we accompanied it with a narrative of the commentaries. We will only aver that as a result of this burning, Spiritism experienced an unexpected growth throughout Spain, and just as the Spirits had predicted, it won over an incalculable number of followers. Thus, like Allan Kardec, we can only rejoice at the great advertisement of this hateful act on behalf of Spiritism. By the way, however, concerning the advertising that we ourselves must do on behalf of our philosophy, we must never forget the master's advice (*Revue Spirite*, 1863, p. 367):

"Spiritism is meant for those who do not believe or who have doubts; not to those who have faith and for whom their faith is sufficient. It tells no one to renounce his or her beliefs in order to adopt ours; this is consonant with the principles of tolerance and freedom of conscience that it professes. For this reason, we cannot approve of attempts by certain individuals to convert the clergy to our ideas, no matter what spiritual community they belong to. Hence, we will repeat to all Spiritists: Use kindness to welcome persons of goodwill; offer the light only to those who are seeking it, for you will not be very successful with those who already believe; do not impose (your) faith on anyone, especially regarding the clergy as opposed to the laity, for you will be sowing barren fields; make the light evident so that it may be seen by those who want to see it; show the fruit of the tree and give it to the ones who are hungry and not to those who say they are sated." This advice, like all of Kardec's recommendations, is clear, simple and especially practical. It will behoove us to remember it and opportunely heed it.

* * *

The year 1862 was fertile for doing the work of spreading Spiritism. On January 15, a small, excellent advertising brochure appeared, entitled: *Spiritism in its Simplest Expression*. "The aim of this publication," said Kardec, "is to present a highly summarized outline, a history of Spiritism and a sufficient enough idea of the Spirits' doctrine to enable its moral and philosophical purpose to be understood. Through the clarity and simplicity of its style, we have sought to place it within reach of all levels of intelligence. We are counting on the devotion of all true Spiritists to help disseminate it." This appeal was heard, for the short brochure spread far and wide, and many people credited this excellent work for their being able to understand the purpose and scope of Spiritism.

On January 1, 1862, after receiving expressions of gratitude and respect from Lyon Spiritists through nearly 200 people's signatures, Allan Kardec sent the following response to all Spiritists in France and abroad:

"My dear brothers and friends of Lyon:

"Your expressions of gratitude, which you were so kind to send to me on New Year's Day, gave me great satisfaction; it shows that you have kept a good memory of me. However, what brought me even greater pleasure regarding your spontaneous act was in finding so many signatures representing nearly every group since it is a sign of the harmony reigning among them. I am happy to see that you have perfectly understood the aim of this organization, whose results you can already appreciate, for by now it should be obvious to you that a single society would be almost impossible. My good friends, I am thankful for your wishes; these are the ones to which God listens. You can rest assured that he hears you every day, providing me with extraordinary satisfaction in the establishing of a new doctrine, and in seeing the one to which I have devoted myself grow and prosper during my lifetime with marvelous speed. I regard it as a great favor from heaven to be a witness to the good that it has already produced. This fact, of which I receive the most touching testimonies daily, has paid me back with interest for all my hardships, all my weariness. I ask God for one favor only: that he may give me the necessary physical strength to complete my task, which is still far from being fulfilled. But whatever happens, I will always have great consolation in the fact that the seed of these new ideas, now spread everywhere, is imperishable. I have been happier than many others who have only worked for the future, while I myself have been allowed to see the first fruits. If I have one thing to regret, it is that the scantiness of my personal resources has not allowed me to carry out the plans that I conceived for an even faster advance. However, if God in his wisdom has decided its course to be otherwise, I will bequeath my plans to our successors, who undoubtedly will be more fortunate. In spite of the scarcity of material resources, the movement has surpassed all expectations; believe me, my brothers, your example in the process will not have been without influence. Thus, please accept our congratulations for the way in which you have come to understand and practice the Doctrine.

"At the point to which things have arrived today, and having in mind the forward progress of Spiritism across the obstacles that have been sown along its way, one can state that the main problems have been overcome; it has won its place and is seated on bases that from now on will challenge the efforts of its adversaries. People wonder how a doctrine that makes us happier and better could have enemies; that is natural: the establishment of better things always shocks people's interests at first. Has not the same thing happened with all the inventions and discoveries that have revolutionized industry? Have not those that nowadays are regarded as beneficial and without which we could no longer live had their stubborn enemies? Is not every law that restrains abuse opposed by those who live by such abuse? How could you expect a doctrine that leads to the kingdom of effective charity not to be fought against by all those who live in selfishness? And you know how innumerable they are on the earth! At first, they tried to kill it with scorn; nowadays, they can see that this weapon is powerless and that under the fire of sarcasm, it has unhesitatingly proceeded on its way. Do not believe that they have conceded defeat, however; no, material interest is tenacious. Since they realize that it is a power that they must face from now on, they have begun to direct more serious assaults against it, but these will only serve to better attest to their own weaknesses. Some will attack it directly with words and deeds, and will even persecute its followers, whom they will make every effort to dishearten through harassment, whereas others will secretly and disguisedly try to undermine it. Do not think that the fight has ended. I have been advised that they will make a supreme effort. Do not be afraid, however. The banner of victory is in the motto proclaimed by all true Spiritists: *Without charity there is no salvation.* Hoist it high, for it is the Medusa's head for selfish individuals. The tactic that has been used by Spiritism's enemies up till now, but which they are about to employ with renewed ardor, is to try to divide Spiritists by creating divergent theories and arousing distrust and jealousy amongst them. Do not fall into their trap. You can be sure that whoever looks for a means – whatever it may be – to disrupt good harmony cannot have good intentions. That is why I recommend that you use the utmost circumspection when you form your groups, not only for your own peace-of-mind but also in the interest of your endeavors.

"*The nature of Spiritist work requires composure and concentration* and the latter is impossible if one is preoccupied with arguments and with displays of malevolent sentiments. There will be no malevolent sentiments where there is fraternity, but there can be no fraternity where there is selfishness, ambition and pride. Among the proud, who are susceptible to being offended by everything, the ambitious, who feel mortified if they are not in charge, and the selfish, who think of no one but themselves, schism is not far off, and with it, dissolution. That is exactly what our enemies want, and it is precisely what they are trying to create. If a group wants to be orderly, tranquil and stable, the sentiment of fraternity must reign. Any group or society that forms without having effective charity as its foundation will have no vitality, whereas those that are founded according to the true spirit of the Doctrine will see their members as being of the same family, albeit not living under the same roof. Any rivalry among them would be nonsense; it could not exist where true charity reigns, for charity cannot be understood in two different ways. Hence, *recognize true Spiritists in the charity of their thoughts, words and deeds*, and know that those who nourish sentiments of animosity, rancor, hatred, envy or jealousy in their souls in fact lie to themselves and only pretend to understand and practice Spiritism. Selfishness and pride kill individual societies just as they kill cultures and society in general…"

All such just and practical advice would deserve being quoted, but we must limit ourselves due to the time at our disposal. At the request of the Spiritists in Lyon and Bordeaux, Allan Kardec took a long advertising excursion in September and October, sowing the Good News everywhere, and offering advice only to those who asked for it. The invitation from the Lyon groups was signed by five hundred individuals. A special publication reported on this excursion of more than six weeks, during which the master presided over more than fifty meetings in twenty cities, where he was always warmly received and felt fortunate to observe the huge progress of Spiritism. Regarding Kardec's trips, since certain hostile influences had spread the rumor that the trips were taken at the expense of the Parisian Society for Spiritist Studies, from whose budget he withdrew beforehand all his expenses for correspondence and maintenance, the master thus refuted this falsity:

"A lot of people, especially in the province, thought that the costs for these trips were covered by the Parisian Society. We had to undo that error when the opportunity arose; to those who still share this belief, we will remind them of what we affirmed on another occasion (*Revue Spirite*, June, 1862, p. 167), that is, the Society limits itself to covering only its current expenses and possesses no reserves. For it to be able to accumulate capital, it would have to aim at numbers, and that is what it does not do, nor does it want to, because its purpose is not speculation; numbers add nothing to the importance of its work. The Society's influence is completely moral and that is the characteristic of its meetings, which give outsiders the idea of a grave and serious gathering. That is its most powerful means of advertising. Thus, it could not provide for such expenses. The expenses for the trip, like all those which our relationships entail for Spiritism, were taken from our personal resources and savings, supplemented with profit from our books, without which it would be impossible for us to meet all the expenses that are the consequence of the work we have undertaken. This is stated without vanity and solely to pay homage to the truth, and is for the edification of those who believe that we amass capital."

In 1862 Kardec also published a *Refutation of the Criticisms against Spiritism*, from the point of view of materialism, science and religion.[8]

In April of 1864, he published *The Imitation of the Gospel according to Spiritism*, which explained the moral maxims of Christ, their application and their harmonization with Spiritism. The work's title was later modified and today is simply *The Gospel according to Spiritism*.

Taking advantage of some vacation time, Kardec took a trip in September of 1864 to Antwerp and Brussels. In explaining to the Belgian Spiritists his modus operandi with Spiritist groups and societies, he told them what he had already said in Lyon in 1861: "Thus, it is better to have one hundred groups of ten to twenty adherents in a city, and where no group assumes supremacy over the others, than to have just a single society where everyone meets. This division in no way harms the unity of the members, since they are all under the same banner and all have the same goal as their purpose." Large societies have their reason for being, from an advertising point of view, but as for serious and continuous study, it is preferable for there to be close groups.

On August 1, 1865 Kardec published a new work: *Heaven and Hell or Divine Justice according to Spiritism*, which contained several examples of the situations of spirits both in the spirit world and on the earth, along with the reasons for such situations.

The remarkable success of Spiritism and its almost unbelievable growth created innumerable enemies, and as it grew, Kardec's task grew also. The Master had an iron will and a extraordinary fighting spirit;

---

[8] Actually, in the book *Voyage Spirite* (Ledoyen, Paris, 1862), Kardec says that he gave up on the idea of publishing the booklet that he had announced one year earlier (*Revue Spirite*, Dec. 1861) and which would have been entitled *Réfutation des critiques contre le Spiritisme au point de vue matérialiste, scientifique et religieux.* – Publisher's note.

he was a tireless worker; he was on his feet in all seasons from 4:30 a.m. on, responding to everything: the vehement polemics directed both against Spiritism and himself, the numerous letters addressed to him; he attended to directing *Revue Spirite* and the Parisian Society for Spiritist Studies, organizing Spiritism and preparing its works. This physical and mental excess exhausted his body and the Spirits repeatedly had to reprimand him in order to make him spare his health. However, he knew that he would not last more than ten more years: several communications had warned him of that time limit and told him that he would only conclude his task in a new existence, which would follow the short interval of his coming discarnation. That is why he did not want to waste any opportunity to give Spiritism everything he could in strength and vitality.

In 1867 he took a short trip to Bordeaux, Tours and Orleans; then he once again went to work to publish *Genesis, Miracles and Prophecies according to Spiritism* in January of 1868. This is one of his most important works because it is a synthesis of the first four already-published volumes from a scientific point of view.

Next, Kardec occupied himself with a plan to organize Spiritism, by which he hoped to add more energy and action to the philosophy of which he was the apostle, seeking to develop its practical aspect and to enable it to produce its fruits. The constant object of his preoccupations was to know who would replace him, because he felt that his discarnation was at hand. The constitution he was preparing had precisely the purpose of providing for the future needs of the Spiritist Doctrine.

During the early years of Spiritism and from the income from his pedagogical works, Allan Kardec had bought 2,666 square meters of land on Segur Avenue behind Avenue of the Invalides. Because this purchase had exhausted his resources, he took out a 50,000 franc loan with Credit Foncier in order to build six small houses with a garden on the land. He nourished the sweet hope of retiring to one of them on Vila Segur, and after his death, it would become a rest home for indigent defenders of Spiritism to retire at in old age.

In 1869 the Spiritist Society was reconstituted and became an anonymous society with capital of 40,000 francs, divided into forty shares of 1,000 francs to be used for the bookstore, *Revue Spirite*, and the works of Allan Kardec. This new society was to commence on April 1 at 7 Lille St. Kardec, whose lease on Sainte-Anne was about to expire, planned to move to Vila Segur in order to work more actively on the books he still had to write, and whose layout and documentation had already been put in order. Thus, he was fully ready to change residences when on March 31 the heart disease that had silently undermined him put an end to his robust constitution, and like a lightning bolt, took him from the affection of his disciples. This was a great loss to Spiritism, which saw its founder and most powerful propagator disappear, and it threw all those who had known and loved him into profound consternation.

"Hippolyte-Leon-Denizard Rivail – Allan Kardec – died in Paris at 59 Sainte-Anne, 2nd District and *mairie* de la Banque, on March 31, 1869 at 65 years of age after succumbing to an aneurism."

The grievous news was received with unanimous sentiments and a huge crowd accompanied the mortal remains of the one who had been Allan Kardec – the one who shone like a burning meteorite at the dawn of Spiritism – to their final resting place at Pere-Lachaise.

Four eulogies were proffered at the mouth of the Master's tomb: the first by Mr. Levent on behalf of the Parisian Spiritist Society; the second by Mr. Camille Flammarion, who not only sketched an outline of Allan Kardec's character and the role that his works performed in the contemporary movement, but also, and especially, an examination of the situation of the physical sciences from the point of view of the invisible world, the unknown natural forces, and the existence of the soul and its indestructibility. Next, Mr. Alexandre Delanne spoke on behalf of Spiritists from out-of-town centers, and, finally, Mr. E. Muller, on behalf of Kardec's family and friends, said the last goodbyes to the dearly departed.

Mrs. Kardec was 74 years old at the time of her husband's passing. She lived until 1883, when on January 21 she passed away at the age of 89 without any direct heirs.

It would be a mistake for anyone to believe that judging from the nature of his works, Allan Kardec must have always been a cold and austere person. That was not the case. After having discussed the most difficult points of psychology and transcendental metaphysics, this serious philosopher would show his cheerful side and would go to great lengths to entertain his frequent guests at Vila Segur. He was always dignified and sober in his manners and knew how to season them with our old Gallic salt through fiery flashes of wit and affable kindness. He loved to laugh with that frank, slow and communicative melodious laugh, and had a particular talent in enabling others to share in his good humor.

All the newspapers of the time concerned themselves with the death of Allan Kardec, and they tried to surmise its consequences. Following is what Mr. Pages de Noyez wrote in the *Journal de Paris* of April 3, 1869:

"He, who for so long occupied the scientific and religious world under the pseudonym Allan Kardec, was called Rivail and died at the age of 65. We saw him lying on a simple mattress in the middle of the session room in which he had presided for so many years. We saw him with the peaceful look expressed by those to whom death has come as no surprise, those who are at peace for having lived an honest life filled with work and who display a reflection of purity that their soul has stamped on their abandoned body.

"Resigned through faith in a better life and through the conviction of the immortality of the soul, many disciples have cast a last glance to those discolored lips, which, only the day before, spoke the language of the earth. But they have already received the consolation of life beyond the grave: Allan Kardec's spirit came to tell them what his state of confusion had been, his first impressions, and who, from among his predecessors in the after life, had come to help his soul detach itself from matter. If 'style makes the man' then those who knew Allan Kardec in life cannot help being moved by the authenticity of that spirit communication.

"Allan Kardec's death is noteworthy due to a strange coincidence. The Society founded by that great popularizer of Spiritism had simply disappeared. The place had been abandoned and all the furniture removed. Nothing remained of a past that was to be reborn on new foundations. At the end of the last session, the president said his goodbyes; his mission completed, he withdrew from the daily struggle in order to devote himself entirely to studying spiritualist philosophy. Others, who are younger – intrepid individuals – would continue his work and strong in their virility, impose the truth by their conviction.

"Why refer to the details of his death? Why does the way the instrument broke matter? Why devote a line to those fragments from here onward immersed in the immense vortex of molecules? Allan Kardec died at the proper time. With him ended the prolog to a living religion, which, radiating outward everyday, will soon have illumined all humankind. No one better than Kardec could have fulfilled the work of spreading Spiritism, and for which it was necessary to sacrifice long vigils that nourished the spirit, to have the patience that educates with the passing of time, and the self-denial that confronts the folly of the present in order to see nothing except the radiance of the future. With his works, Allan Kardec has founded the dogma foretold by the most ancient societies. His name, appreciated as that of a moral man, has long been popularized by those who believe and those who fear. It is difficult to practice the good without shocking established interests. Spiritism destroys many abuses and uplifts many sorrowful consciences, giving them the certainty of the proof and consolation of the future.

"Spiritists today mourn the friend who has left them because our understanding, which is material, so to speak, cannot submit itself to the idea of *transition*; however, once the first tribute to this inferiority of our organism is paid, we lift our head and cross over into that invisible world which we feel exists beyond the grave, and we reach out our hand to the friend who is no longer with us, convinced that his spirit will always watch over us. The president of the Parisian Spiritist Society is dead, but the number of followers grows day by day, and the courageous ones, those who through their respect for the master held themselves back, will not hesitate to assert themselves for the good of the great cause. This death, which the common folk have regarded with indifference, is nevertheless a great event for humankind. It is no longer the tomb of a man; it is the tombstone filling that immense emptiness that materialism had carved out at our feet and upon which Spiritism has scattered flowers of hope."

One point that does not attract our attention, but which should be pointed out, is the true Christian charity of Allan Kardec. One could say that his left hand never knew the good his right hand was doing, and that this one never knew the bites made at the other by those for whom gratitude is an excessively heavy burden. Anonymous letters, insults, betrayals and systematic defamations - nothing was spared this intrepid fighter, this great and heroic soul who has fully entered immortality.

Allan Kardec's mortal remains rest in Pere-Lachaise in Paris under the modest headstone set up by the piety of his disciples. It is at this place that, since 1869, followers who have faithfully guarded the memory of the Master and who have preciously kept him in their hearts gather every year.

And since we are reunited by an analogous sentiment, let us repeat out loud, ladies and gentlemen:

Blessed be Allan Kardec!

Henri Sausse.

---

* (footnote) – Abridged version of Henry Sausse's speech presented on March 31, 1896, when Lyon Spiritists celebrated Allan Kardec's 27th discarnation anniversary. Full text *Biographie d' Allan Kardec,* Henri Sausse.

WHAT IS SPIRITISM?

Prologue

Persons who have only a superficial understanding of Spiritism will, of course, be led to ask certain questions about it, and a thorough study would certainly provide the answers. However, these individuals often lack the time and frequently the willpower to undertake an ongoing study. Before doing so, they will at least want to know what they are dealing with and if it is worthwhile to concern themselves with it. Therefore, it seemed to us that it would be useful to provide in a concise form the answers to some of the fundamental questions that are asked of us every day. For the reader, this will comprise a preliminary initiation, and for us, it will save us from constantly having to repeat the same things.

The first chapter uses dialogue form to answer the most common objections of those who are unaware of the Doctrine's primary fundamentals, as well as to refute the main arguments of its opponents. This format seemed the most suitable because it does not involve the dryness of the dogmatic form.

The second chapter is devoted to a succinct exposition of the science's practical and experimental aspects, to which, in the absence of a complete study, novice observers should direct their attention with full knowledge of the facts. In a way, this chapter forms a summary of *The Mediums' Book*. Most often, objections arise from preconceived, wrong ideas concerning something one does not understand. To rectify such ideas means to anticipate the objections: such is the goal of this little section.

The third chapter may be regarded as a summary of *The Spirits' Book*, which contains the Spiritist Doctrine's solution to a number of problems of great psychological, moral and philosophical interest, problems posed daily and for which no philosophy has yet provided any satisfactory solution. If we try to solve them using some other theory and without the key that Spiritism furnishes, we will realize that Spiritism's answers are still the most logical and those that better satisfy reason.

This summary is useful not only for beginners who will be able to draw the essential notions of Spiritism from it in a short amount of time and without much effort, but also for its adherents because it will furnish them the means to respond to the main objections that will never cease to be raised, and because they will find here at a glance and under a concise form the principles that they must never lose sight of.

In order to respond summarily here and now to the question formulated in the title of this short work, we will state that:

Spiritism is simultaneously a science of observation and a philosophical doctrine. As a practical science, it consists in the relations that can be established with spirits. As a philosophy, it entails all the moral consequences that result from such relations.

Hence, it may be defined as follows:

Spiritism is a science that deals with the nature, origin and destiny of spirits, and their relation with the corporeal world.

Chapter I

A Brief Discussion of Spiritism

First dialogue

The critic

A Visitor – I must tell you, sir, that my reason refuses to accept the reality of the strange phenomena attributed to spirits, which I am convinced exist only in the imagination. However, one would have to bow down before the evidence and that is what I will do if presented with uncontestable proof. Hence, not wanting to impose, I have come to ask for your kind permission to watch just one or two experiments in order to be convinced if possible.

Allan Kardec – Well, if your reason refuses to accept what we consider to be established facts, it is because you believe it to be superior to the reason of all other persons who do not share your opinion. I have no doubts about your worthiness, nor would I claim that my own intelligence is greater than yours. So, let's accept the fact that I am in the wrong – since your reason says that I am – and therefore there is nothing more to be said on the matter.

Visitor – Nevertheless, I am widely recognized as an opponent of your ideas, and if you were to convince me, it would be a miracle eminently favorable to your cause.

A.K. – I'm sorry, sir, but I don't have the gift of performing miracles. Do you really think that one or two sessions would be enough to convince you? That indeed would be a *tour de force*. It took more than a year of study for me to become convinced, which goes to show that if I now am, it was not done thoughtlessly. Besides, I don't offer public sessions and it seems that you may be mistaken about the purpose of our meetings, since we do not perform experiments in order to satisfy people's curiosity.

Visitor – So you do not try to win converts?

A.K. – Why would I want to win you over as convert if you do not want to become one? I can't make anyone believe. When I meet individuals who sincerely desire to learn, and who give me the honor of asking for explanations, it is my pleasure and duty to respond to them within the limits of my knowledge. However, as for opponents who, like yourself, are set in their ways, I do not make any effort to dissuade them because I can find plenty of persons who are willing to be convinced. I don't have to waste my time on those who are not. Conviction will inevitably come sooner or later, and the most disbelieving will be swept along by the current. For now, a few more or a few less adherents will not tip the scales. That is why you will never see me worrying about attracting to our ideas those who, like yourself, have such good reasons to keep their distance from them.

Visitor – Nevertheless, there could be more interest in convincing me than you might think. Would you allow me to explain myself honestly and promise me that you won't be offended? These are my thoughts on the matter itself and not the person I'm addressing. I can respect the person without having to share his opinion.

A.K. – Spiritism has taught me to place little value on the petty susceptibilities of self-esteem, and not to feel offended by mere words. If your statements overstep the limits of civility and propriety, I will conclude that you are an impolite person, that's all. As for myself, I prefer to leave others in their errors instead of sharing in them. So, from that alone you can see that Spiritism is good for something.

As I have already stated, I have no intention of making you share my opinion. I respect yours if it is sincere, just as I want you to respect mine. Because you treat Spiritism as a hollow dream, you must have said to yourself on your way here: "I'm going to see a lunatic." Admit it frankly, I won't be upset. That all Spiritists are crazy is an established thing. Fine, then! Since you regard this as a mental illness, I would feel guilty in transmitting it to you, and I'm surprised that with such a thought in mind you would seek to acquire a conviction that would place you amongst lunatics. If you were persuaded beforehand that you cannot be convinced, your effort is futile since its only objective is curiosity. So I ask of you, let's be brief, because I don't have time to waste on pointless conversations.

Visitor – But a person can be mistaken and deluded without being crazy because of it.

A.K. – To put it plainly, you are saying, like so many others, that Spiritism is a fad whose time will pass. But you must agree that a fad, which has taken only a few years to win millions of adherents in every country, which includes learned individuals of every order amongst its followers, and which is spreading especially amongst the educated classes, is a peculiar mania that is worthy of a little examination.

Visitor – True, I do have my own ideas on the matter; however, they are not so unyielding that I wouldn't be willing to sacrifice them to the evidence. That is why I said that you might have a certain interest in convincing me. I must confess that I plan to publish a book, in which I propose to demonstrate *ex professo*[9] what I regard as an error. The book would have a far-reaching impact and deal a blow to the Spirits, but if I were to be convinced otherwise, I won't publish it.

A.K. – I would feel awful if I were to deprive you of the profits from a book that must be so far-reaching. Besides, I have no interest in keeping you from publishing it; on the contrary,

---

9 Expressly. – Tr.

I hope it will be well-received, because it will serve to publicize and advertise us. When something is attacked, attention is drawn to it; there are a lot of people who like to see its pros and cons, and criticism makes it known to those who hadn't even thought about it. That is why often, and without meaning to, publicity ends up benefiting those it was meant to harm. Moreover, the issue of spirits is so interesting and arouses so much curiosity that it is enough to merely draw attention to it and people will want to examine it more profoundly.[10]

Visitor – So, in your opinion, criticism is useless and public opinion doesn't count for anything?

A.K. – I don't regard criticism as an expression of public opinion, but as a personal opinion that may be mistaken. Look at history and you will see how many masterpieces were criticized when they first appeared; but that did not keep them from being masterpieces. When something is bad, all the praise in the world will not make it good. *If Spiritism is an error, it will fall by itself; if it is a truth, all the diatribes in the world will not render it a lie.* Your book will be a personal appraisal from your own point of view – true public opinion will decide whether or not you are right. Thus, people will want to examine the matter for themselves, and if they realize that you were wrong, your book will be ridiculed like the one published not too long ago against the theories on the circulation of the blood, on vaccine, etc.

But I have forgotten that you are going to treat the issue *ex professo*, which means that you have studied it from every angle; that you have seen all there is to see and have read everything that has been written on the matter; that you have analyzed and compared all the different opinions; that you were in the best position to observe for yourself; that you have dedicated your

---

[10] After this dialogue, written in 1859, experience largely proved the correctness of this proposition. – Tr.

waking hours to the subject for years; in other words, that you have neglected nothing to arrive at the truth. I must believe that you have done so if you are a trustworthy person, because only one who has done all those things has the right to say that he speaks with full knowledge of the facts.

What would you think of someone who claimed to be a critic of a literary work but who had no knowledge of literature, or of a painting but who had never studied art? It's only logical that critics must understand, not superficially but in depth, what they are discussing; otherwise, their opinion is worthless. To disprove a calculation, one must oppose it with another calculation, but in order to do so one must know how to calculate. Critics must not limit themselves to saying that a certain thing is good or bad. They must justify their opinion with a clear and categorical demonstration based on the very principles of art or science. How can they do so if they do not know what such principles are? Could you evaluate the qualities or defects of a machine if you didn't know anything about mechanics? No, you couldn't. Well then! Since you know nothing about Spiritism, your opinion would be no more valuable than your opinion about that machine. At each step you would be caught in your ignorance, because those who have studied Spiritism would see right away that you are not knowledgeable on the matter, which would lead them to conclude either that you are not serious or that you are acting in bad faith. In either case, you would be exposing yourself to being disavowed, which would hardly be flattering to your self-esteem.

Visitor – It is precisely to avoid such a pitfall that I have come to ask you to allow me to watch a few experiments.

A.K. – And you think that that would be enough for you to be able to speak *ex professo* about Spiritism? How could you comprehend such experiments – let alone judge them – if you haven't studied the principles upon which they are based? How could you rightly or wrongly evaluate the result of metallurgical experiments, for instance, if you don't even know the fundamentals of metallurgy? Allow me to say that your plan is exactly the same as if, in spite of knowing neither mathematics nor astronomy, you were to say to one of the members of the Observatory: "Sir, I would like to write a book on astronomy, and what is more, I would like to prove that your theory is wrong. But since I don't know the first thing about the science, I need you to let me look through your telescope once or twice. That should be enough for me to know as much about it as you do."

It is only by extension that the verb *to critique* becomes synonymous with the verb *to censure*. In its proper meaning and according to its etymology, the term *to critique* means *to judge*, *to appraise;* hence, a critique may be approving or disapproving. To critique a book is not necessarily to condemn it. Those who undertake the job should do so without any preconceived ideas. But if they have already condemned the book in their minds before having even opened it, their appraisal cannot be impartial.

Such is the case with the majority of those who have spoken about Spiritism. They formed an opinion based solely on the name, and they proceeded like a judge who has passed sentence without having taken the time to study the documentary evidence. The result was that their judgment was incorrect, and instead of being persuasive, they aroused scorn. As for those who seriously studied the subject, most changed their mind, and a good number of adversaries became adherents once they realized it was something different from what they had thought.

Visitor – You speak of the appraisal of books in general. Do you really think it is materially possible for journalists to read and study everything that passes through their hands, especially if it deals with new theories that require their in-depth verification? That would be like requiring printers to read all the books that leave their presses.

A.K. – In light of such judicious reasoning I have nothing to answer, except that, if one does not have the time to do something conscientiously, one should not get involved with it, and that it is better to do only one thing well than ten things badly.

Visitor – Please don't think that I arrived at my opinion lightly. I have seen tables turn and produce raps; I have seen persons who were supposedly writing under the influence of spirits. Nevertheless, I'm convinced that charlatanism was involved.

A.K. – And how much did you pay?

Visitor – Why, nothing, of course.

A.K. – Well, they must have been an odd breed of charlatans and they will give a new meaning to the word. Until now, no one has ever seen a charlatan who wasn't in it for the money. If some mischievous hoaxer happened to want to entertain himself once, would it follow that other persons were in association with him? Moreover, what would they hope to gain by being accomplices to a hoax? To amuse people, you will say. I will admit that someone might pull a hoax once, but if a hoax goes on for months and even years, I would say that it is the hoaxer who is being duped. Would someone sit tediously at a table for hours on end for the sheer pleasure of making others believe in something he or she knows to be false? The pleasure would not be worth the effort.

Before concluding that something is a fraud, we must first ask ourselves what might be gained from such deceit. You will agree that there are situations that exclude all suspicion of fraud and that there are individuals whose character alone is a guarantee of honesty.

It would be a different matter if it involved speculation, because the attraction of profit is a bad advisor. However, even if we were to accept the fact that in such a case a fraudulent operation might be entirely possible, it would prove nothing against the reality of the principle, because anything can be misused. Just because there are persons who sell adulterated wines, that doesn't mean that there is no such thing as pure wine. Spiritism is no more responsible for those who misuse its name and exploit it than medical science is responsible for the charlatans who sell their snake oils or religion for the clergy who abuse their ministry.

Due to its newness and its very nature, Spiritism may lend itself to abuses. However, it has provided the means of recognizing them by clearly defining its true character and by refusing to have anything to do with those who exploit it or divert it from its exclusively moral objective in order to make it a trade, an instrument of divination or pointless experimentation.

Since Spiritism sets its owns boundaries, determines what it says and what it doesn't say, what it can and what it cannot do, what attributes it does or doesn't entail, and what it accepts and what it rejects, the error lies with those who, not having put forth the effort to study it, judge it by appearances, and because they have met entertainers employing the name *Spiritist* in order to attract passers-by, they gravely state, "This is what Spiritism is." In the end, upon whom does ridicule fall? Not upon the entertainers, who are only performing their act, nor upon Spiritism, whose written doctrine belies such assertions. It falls upon convinced critics, who either talk about what they do not know, or who consciously twist the truth. Those who attribute to Spiritism what is contrary to its very essence do so either out of ignorance or deliberately. As for the former, it is thoughtlessness; as for the latter, it is bad faith. In the latter case, they resemble certain historians, who, in the interest of a party or an opinion, twist the historical facts. A party always discredits itself by employing such means, and will fail to reach its objective.

Please take note of the fact that I don't mean that critics must necessarily approve of our ideas, even after having studied them. We in no way reproach those who do not think as we do.

What is obvious to us might not be to everybody else. People judge matters from their own point of view, and not all draw the same conclusions from the most obvious facts. For example, if a painter puts a white horse in his painting, someone might very well say that the horse produces a bad effect, that a black one would have been more suitable. It would be an error, however, to state that the horse is white when it is black – which is exactly what most of our adversaries do.

To sum it all up, people are perfectly free to approve of or criticize the principles of Spiritism, to deduce the good or bad consequences from them as they please; however, conscience imposes a duty on every trustworthy critic not to state the opposite of what Spiritism is. Thus, the first requirement of being a critic is not to talk about things one knows nothing about.

Visitor – Could we go back to the moving and talking tables? Mightn't they have been rigged beforehand?

A.K. – It's the same question of good faith, and I have already answered it. The second that fraud is demonstrated, I will be the first to admit it to you. If you can point out *confirmed* incidents of fraud, charlatanism, exploitation or abuse of trust, I will deliver them to your whip, and I'll tell you right now that I'll not take up their defense, since real Spiritism is the first to repudiate them. Pointing out such abuses helps to prevent them and renders a service to Spiritism. But to generalize such accusations, to cast over a large number of respectable individuals the reproof that only a few isolated individuals deserve is an abuse of a different sort – it is slander.

Even if we were to suppose that the tables had been rigged, there would have to be a sufficiently ingenious mechanism to make them produce such varied movements and noises. But why hasn't anyone found out who the skillful manufacturer is that builds them? He should be enjoying great fame by now since his devices are scattered all over the five continents. We also must agree that his technique is highly ingenious since it can be successfully adapted to the first table at hand without any exterior traces. Why is it that from Tertullian[11] – who spoke of turning and talking tables – down to the present, no one has ever seen or described such a mechanism?

Visitor – You are mistaken. A well-known surgeon has discovered that when certain individuals contract a tendon in their leg, they can produce a noise similar to what you attribute to the tables, from which he concluded that your mediums entertain themselves at the expense of others' gullibility.[12]

A.K. – Well, if it's the tendon that crackles, then it's not the table that has been rigged. Since everyone explains this so-called fraud in their own way, that in itself is the most obvious proof that neither they nor anyone else knows the true cause.

I respect the erudition of this learned surgeon; however there are a number of problems with applying his theory to the talking tables. First, until now, this ability has been regarded as exceptional and has been seen as pathological, and it's remarkable that it has suddenly become so common. Second, one would have to have a profound desire to deceive to warrant crackling one's tendon for two or three hours straight because it produces nothing but pain and fatigue. Third, I can't see how the tendon makes contact with the doors and walls in which raps have been heard. Fourth and finally, the crackling tendon would have to be endowed with the marvelous ability of moving a heavy table, lifting it and keeping it suspended in the air without any point of support, and then finally smashing it back onto the floor. Certainly, no one could have dreamed that this tendon had so many abilities![13]

Did the celebrated surgeon of whom you are speaking study the phenomenon of typtology in those who produce it? No. He

---

[11] Late second, early third century theologian. – Tr.

[12] For further treatment of the "Crackling Tendon Theory," see *The Mediums' Book*, pt. 1, chap. IV, no. 41. – Tr.

[13] *Revue Spirite*, June of 1859, p. 141, "Le muscle craqueur." – Auth.

observed an abnormal physiological condition in a few individuals who had never even concerned themselves with rapping tables. After having drawn a certain analogy between this condition and the effect produced by the tables, he didn't bother with a more in-depth examination, and using all the authority of his knowledge, he concluded that all who cause tables to talk must possess the ability to crack the short peroneal tendon, and that they are nothing more than tricksters, whether they are princes or artisans, and whether they receive payment or not. Did he at least study the phenomenon of typtology in all its expressions? Did he check to see if every one of the typtological effects could be produced by means of this crackling tendon? If he had, he would have been convinced of the insufficiency of his approach. But that didn't keep him from proclaiming his discovery to the Institute. For a scholar, he really expounded quite a serious conclusion! And what has become of him? I must confess that if I had to have surgery, I would be very hesitant to entrust myself to this practitioner because I would be afraid that he hadn't diagnosed my problem with any more precision than he did in this case.

Since his opinion is one of the authorities upon which you want to support your attack against Spiritism, it gives me a good idea of the strength of your other arguments, if they have not been drawn from a more reliable source.

Visitor – Nonetheless, you can see that the turning table fad has passed; it was all the rage for a while, but nowadays no one cares about it anymore. Why not, if it has to do with such a serious matter?

A.K. – Because the turning tables led to something even more serious; they led to an entire science, an entire philosophical doctrine, which is of much greater interest for thinking individuals. When they no longer had any more to learn by watching tables turn, they were no longer concerned about them. For frivolous persons, who do not delve more deeply into anything, they were a pastime, a game that they put aside once they had had enough. Such individuals are not taken into account by science. The time of curiosity had its day; the time of observation followed. Spiritism has thus entered the realm of serious individuals, who do not entertain themselves with it but seek enlightenment. Moreover, persons who regard it as a serious matter do not lend themselves to any experiment out of mere curiosity, and even less to persons who would approach it with hostile thoughts. Since they do not amuse themselves, they do not try to amuse others; I count myself among them.

Visitor–Even so, nothing is as convincing as experimentation, even if at first its purpose is mere curiosity. If you operate solely in the presence of persons who are already convinced, allow me to say that you are preaching to the converted.

A.K. – It is one thing to be convinced and another to be willing to be convinced. I address the latter, and not those who think they are humiliating their reason by coming to hear about what they call reveries; I concern myself very little with these. As for those who say they have a sincere desire to be enlightened, the best way they can prove it is by demonstrating perseverance. They can be recognized by other signs besides the desire to watch one or two experimental sessions: they are willing to work seriously.

Conviction is acquired only over time, through continual observation and special attention. Spirit phenomena differ essentially from those displayed in the exact sciences: they cannot be produced at will; we must seize them when they occur. Only by observing them a great deal and for a long time can we discover a drove of proofs that are not apparent at first glance, especially if we are not familiar with the conditions in which they might occur, and even more so when we come with a biased attitude. For diligent and thoughtful observers, the proofs abound: for them, a word, an apparently insignificant incident, may be a ray of light, a confirmation. For superficial and one-time observers, for the simply curious, such incidents are nothing. That is why I do not lend myself to experiments without plausible results.

Visitor – But everything must start somewhere, after all. As for beginners, who are blank slates, who have not seen anything but who want to be enlightened, what can they do if you do not provide the means?

A.K. – I make a big distinction between the disbeliever out of ignorance and the systematic disbeliever. Whenever I see individuals with a favorable disposition, it takes me very little to enlighten them. However, there are individuals whose desire to learn is only a pretense. They are a waste of time because if they do not immediately find what they seem to be looking for and what would perhaps displease them if they did find it, the little they do see isn't enough to erase their prejudices. It's a futile endeavor because they draw the wrong conclusions and make it an object of ridicule.

I will say to someone who truly wants to learn: "One cannot take a course in experimental Spiritism as if it were a course in physics and chemistry, because spirit phenomena cannot be produced at will, and the intelligences that are their agents often thwart all our expectations. What you might see by chance without presenting continuity or any necessary connection will be of little understanding to you. So learn the theory first; read and ponder the literature that deals with this science. That is where you can learn the principles; you'll find a description of all the phenomena and you'll understand their plausibility by the explanation that is provided and by the accounts of a large number of spontaneous phenomena, which you yourself might have witnessed without knowing it, and which will come back to your memory. You will brace yourself against all the problems that might surface, and you will thus form a preliminary moral conviction. Then, when the circumstances arise to observe or act by yourself, you'll understand them unhampered by the order in which the phenomena occur because nothing will be strange to you."

That, sir, is what I advise all who say they want to learn, and by their response it is easy to tell if they are motivated by something other than mere curiosity.

Second Dialogue

The Skeptic

Visitor – Sir, I can understand the usefulness of the preparatory study of which you have just spoken. As for my own personal predisposition, I am neither for nor against Spiritism, but the subject per se has awakened a great deal of interest in me. Within the circle of my acquaintances, there are adherents but there are adversaries too. In this regard, I have heard the most contradicting arguments. I would like to submit to you some of the objections made in my presence, and which seem to have some value to them, at least for me, because I must confess my own ignorance on the matter.

Allan Kardec – It will be a pleasure, sir, to answer your questions if they are sincere and hide no ulterior motives, although I wouldn't flatter myself by thinking I'm capable of answering all of them. Spiritism is a newborn science, about which there is still much to learn. So, it would be quite presumptuous on my part to presume that I could solve every problem: I can tell you only what I know.

Spiritism touches on all branches of philosophy, metaphysics, psychology and morality. It is an immense field that cannot be traversed in a few hours. Thus, you will understand, sir, that it would be materially impossible for me to repeat orally and to each person individually everything I have written for public use on the matter. Moreover, upon a serious preliminary reading of the literature, you will find an answer to most of the questions that may naturally come to mind. Such a reading would have the two-fold advantage of avoiding needless repetitions and of demonstrating a sincere desire to learn. Afterward, if there are still any questions or obscure points, explaining them would be much easier because then we would have a point of reference and would not waste our time going over the most elementary principles again. So if you would allow it, we will limit ourselves to a few general questions for now.

Visitor – Agreed, but I would ask you to call me back to the subject if I happen to wander off it.

Spiritism and Spiritualism

Visitor – To start with, why was it necessary to create the new terms *Spiritist* and *Spiritism* to replace *spiritualist* and *spiritualism*, which are part of everyday speech and well understood by everybody? I understand that some view these new terms as barbarisms.[14]

A.K. – The word *spiritualist* has had a well-defined acceptation for a long time. The Academy defines it in this way: a *SPIRITUALIST is someone whose doctrine is contrary to materialism*. All religions are necessarily based on spiritualism. Whoever believes that there is something within us besides matter is a *spiritualist*; however, that does not imply a belief in spirits or their manifestations. How would you distinguish such a person from one who does believe? You would have to say something like: A spiritualist is someone who might or might not believe in spirits. For new things, new terms are needed if one wants to avoid misunderstandings. If I had classified my REVUE[15] as being *spiritualist*, I would not have been clear about its purpose, since I could very well have not said one word about spirits without

---

[14] *Barbarism:* the use of words or constructions felt to be undesirably alien to the established standards of a language. (*Webster's College Dictionary,* Random House, 1991). For further explanations regarding these terms, see *The Spirits' Book,* Introduction, sect. 1. – Tr.

[15] *Revue Spirite,* published by Kardec from 1858 to 1869. – Tr.

contradicting the title; in fact, I could have been against them altogether. Some time ago I read in a periodical an article of philosophical content stating that the author had written it from a *spiritualist* point of view. However, those who believe in spirits would have been particularly disappointed if, in trusting that description, they had looked for the slightest confirmation of their own ideas. Therefore, if I adopted the terms *Spiritist* and *Spiritism*, it was because they unequivocally express ideas related to spirits. Every *Spiritist* is necessarily a *spiritualist*, but not all *spiritualists* are *Spiritists*. Even if spirits were a mere fancy, it would still be useful to have special terms for matters related to them since terminology is needed as much for erroneous ideas as for correct ones.

Furthermore, these terms are no more barbaric than those that the arts, sciences and industry create each day. They are surely no more improper than those Gall[16] coined for his nomenclature of the faculties, such as: *secretiviness, amativeness, combativeness, alimentiveness, adhesiveness[17],* etc. There are persons who, due to their argumentative nature, criticize anything that they, themselves, have not come up with and thus want to put on airs of opposition to it. Those who insist on such petty squabbles prove only one thing: the shallowness of their ideas. Attacking with such trifles merely shows that they are short on good arguments.

Spiritualism and *spiritualist* are English words used in the United States ever since spirit manifestations first appeared; at first, and for some time thereafter, they were also used in France. However, as soon as the terms *Spiritist* and *Spiritism* appeared, their usefulness was understood and they were immediately accepted by

---

[16] Franz Joseph Gall (1758-1828). German physician and founder of phrenology [sought to establish relationships between mental faculties and skull shape]. Pioneer in ascribing cerebral functions to various areas of the brain (localization); first to identify gray matter of brain with neurons and white matter with ganglia. *Webster's New Biographical Dictionary*. – Tr.

[17] *Elements of Phrenology* – George Combe. – Tr.

the public. Nowadays, their use is so established that even those who at first opposed them and proclaimed them to be barbarisms do not use any others. The sermons and pastoral letters that lash out against *Spiritism* and *Spiritists* would not have been able to cast their anathemas against *spiritualism* and *spiritualists* without bringing confusion to the issue.

Barbarisms or not, the terms *Spiritism* and *Spiritist* have entered everyday usage and all the languages of Europe. They are the only ones used in all publications – pro or con – in every country. They are the backbone of the new science's nomenclature. In order to express the special phenomena of this science, special terms were needed. Spiritism now has its own nomenclature, just as chemistry has its own.[18]

Dissenting Opinions

Visitor – This diversity of belief in what you call a science seems to me to be its undoing. If this science were actually based on provable facts, wouldn't it be identical in both America and Europe?

A.K. – I will first respond that such divergence exists more in form than in essence. In reality, it exists only in the way certain points of the Doctrine are considered, but it does not constitute any radical antagonism concerning the principles, as our adversaries love to say without even having studied the issue.

But tell me: what science is there that, at its start, did not give rise to dissenting opinions until its principles became clearly established? Isn't this dissent still present today in the sciences that have been around much longer? Are all scholars in agreement

---

[18] Moreover, these terms have become more or less bourgeois; they may be found in the supplement to the *Petit Dictionnaire des Dictionnaires Français*, excerpt from *Napoleon Landais*, with a circulation of 20,000 copies. It contains definitions and etymologies of the terms *erraticity, medianimic, medium, mediumship, perispirit, pneumatography, pneumatophony, psychographer, psychography, psychophony, reincarnation, sematology, Spiritist, Spiritism*, and *typtology*. All of these terms may also be found in the new edition of the *Dictionnaire Universel* by Maurice Lachâtre. – Auth.

about the same principle? Don't they all have their particular theories? Do sessions at the Institute always display the picture of perfect and cordial understanding? In medicine, aren't there the Paris School and the Montpellier School? Isn't each discovery in any science cause for schisms between those who want to progress and those who want to remain behind?

Concerning Spiritism, then, wouldn't it be natural that, at the appearance of the first phenomena, when the laws governing them were unknown, everyone would have their own theory and would consider them in a certain way? But what has become of those early isolated theories? They have fallen before a more complete observation of the facts. A few years were enough to establish the magnificent unity that prevails today in the Doctrine, and which brings the great majority of its adherents together, except for a few individuals, who, in this as in all things, cling to primitive ideas and die with them. What science, what philosophical or religious doctrine can offer a similar example? Has Spiritism ever displayed even a hundredth of the schisms that have afflicted the Church over so many centuries, and which still divide it today?

It is truly curious to see the puerilities that Spiritism's adversaries hold on to; doesn't that indicate a lack of good arguments? If they had them, they wouldn't hesitate to use them. So, what do they use to oppose it? Ridicule, denial and slander; but peremptory arguments – none whatsoever. And the proof that they still haven't found a vulnerable angle is that nothing has hindered Spiritism's forward progress, and that after just ten years, it includes more adherents than any sect has ever had after a century in existence. This is a fact taken from experience and recognized even by its adversaries. In order to destroy it, it is not enough to say "this cannot be; this is absurd." It is necessary to prove categorically that the phenomena do not and cannot exist. That is precisely what no one has done.

Simulated Spirit Phenomena

Visitor – Hasn't it been proven that the same phenomena can be produced outside of Spiritism? One may conclude, therefore, that they don't have the origin that Spiritists attribute to them.

A.K. – Simply because something can be imitated, does that mean that it doesn't exist? What would you say about the logic of someone who claimed that, because wine from Champagne is made with seltzer water, all wine from Champagne is nothing but seltzer water? Such is the particular character of all things that can be counterfeited. Illusionists have believed that, due to its popularity and the controversies surrounding it, the name *Spiritism* might be worth exploiting, and in order to attract a crowd, they have more or less crudely simulated a few mediumistic phenomena, just as they used to simulate somnambulistic clairvoyance. And all the scoffers applauded, exclaiming, "Look at what Spiritism is!" When the ingenious production of specters appeared on the scene, didn't they proclaim far and wide that Spiritism had received its mortal blow? Before passing such an assured judgment, they should remember that the assertions of a magician are not the Gospel truth, and they should check to see if there is a true identity between the imitation and the thing imitated. No one buys a diamond before first making sure it's not a rhinestone. A study of the matter, even if not very thorough, would have convinced these scoffers that spirit phenomena occur under completely different conditions, and furthermore, they would have known that Spiritists concern themselves neither with making specters appear nor with fortune-telling.

Only malevolence and remarkable ill will would compare Spiritism to magic and sorcery, since Spiritism repudiates their purpose, practices, formulas and mystical words. There are even those who haven't been afraid to compare Spiritist meetings with

Sabbat gatherings,[19] where people wait for the ominous hour of midnight to make ghosts appear.

One of my Spiritist friends was watching a presentation of *Macbeth* one day seated next to a journalist he did not know. When it was time for the scene with the witches, he overheard the journalist say to his neighbor, "Oh, look! We're going to watch a session of Spiritism. This is exactly what I need for my next article. Now I'm going to see what goes on in them. If there were one of those crazies here, I'd ask him if he recognized himself in this scene." "Well, I'm one of those crazies," said my Spiritist friend, "and I can assure you that I don't see myself in this scene at all because, although I have taken part in hundreds of Spiritist meetings, I haven't found anything like this at any of them. If you have come here to gather material for your article, it will not shine with the truth."

Many critics do not have a more serious basis. On whom does the ridicule fall if not on those who proceed so carelessly? Far from being bruised, Spiritism's credibility has grown because of the publicity that all these ruses have provided by arousing the interest of a crowd of individuals who had never heard of Spiritism. These ploys have prompted the study of it and have increased the number of its adherents because they saw that, instead of a mere game, it was something to be taken quite seriously.

The Powerlessness of Detractors

Visitor – I agree that, among Spiritism's detractors, there are many thoughtless individuals, such as the one you have just mentioned. But alongside them, aren't there some truly worthy persons whose opinions carry a certain weight?

---

[19] Nocturnal gathering of witches, a colorful and intriguing part of the lore surrounding them in Christian European tradition. The concept dates from the mid-14th century when it first appeared in Inquisition records. www.britannica.com. – Tr.

A.K. – I wouldn't deny that at all, but I'll respond by saying that the ranks of Spiritism also contain a good number of individuals who are no less worthy. I'll say further: the overwhelming majority of Spiritists is composed of intelligent and studious persons. Only bad faith would lead anyone to say that they have been recruited from among naive women and the uneducated masses.

Besides, one decisive fact answers this objection: despite their knowledge and official positions, none have managed to hinder Spiritism's progress. Hence, there is no one – even the most obscure pamphlet writer – who has not flattered him or herself for having dealt it a deathblow. Instead, all of them, without exception, have unwittingly helped to popularize it. But doesn't the fact than an idea has resisted such efforts and has advanced undaunted through the hail of blows dealt to it prove its power and the depth of its roots? Doesn't such a phenomenon deserve the attention of serious thinkers? More than a few these days have declared that there must be something to it; that maybe it is one of those great, irresistible movements that shake up societies from time to time in order to transform them.

That is the way it has always been with all the new ideas called upon to revolutionize the world. They run up against obstacles because they have to fight against the very self-interests, prejudices and abuses they have come to overthrow. However, since they are part of God's designs for fulfilling the law of progress for humankind, nothing can stop them when their time comes. It is the proof that they are the expression of truth.

Moreover, as I have already stated, this powerlessness of Spiritism's detractors shows, first of all, an absence of good arguments, since the ones used against it are not convincing. Such powerlessness, however, has to do with another cause that has frustrated all their schemes. They are alarmed by Spiritism's progress, in spite of all they have done to stop it; they have been unable to discover the reason for such progress because they have been looking in all the wrong places. Some have seen it in the great power of the Devil, who would thus show himself stronger than they are, and even stronger than God. Others have regarded it as an increase in human madness. The mistake of all of them is in believing that Spiritism has only one source, and that it rests on the opinion of only one man; thus, they think that if they can ruin this one man, they can ruin Spiritism. They are searching for this source on the earth, whereas it is to be found in the spirit world. It is not in one place; it is everywhere because spirits manifest everywhere, in every country, in the palace as well as the hovel. Hence, the true cause lies in the very nature of Spiritism, which does not receive its impulse from one person only; instead, it allows anyone to receive communications directly from spirits, and thus to be reassured of the reality of the phenomena. How can millions of persons be persuaded that all this is nothing more than conjuration, charlatanism, trickery or a feat of skill, when they themselves can get results without anyone's help? Could they be made to believe that they are their own accomplices and produce deceit and trickery only for their own sake?

The universality of spirit manifestations, which have appeared at all points of the globe to disavow the detractors of Spiritism and to confirm the principles of the Doctrine, is a power that cannot be comprehended by those who know nothing about the invisible world, just as the speed of sending a telegraph message would be incomprehensible to those who know nothing about the law of electricity. It is against this power that all denials have been shattered, because it is like telling persons who receive the rays of the sun that the sun does not exist.

The qualities of the Doctrine notwithstanding – qualities that are more pleasing than the qualities that oppose it – the manifestations are behind the cause of the setbacks of those who have been trying to stop its progress. In order to succeed, they would have to find the means to keep spirits from manifesting. This is why

Spiritists are so unconcerned about their maneuvers: they have the experience and authority of the phenomena on their side.

The Extraordinary and the Supernatural

Visitor – Spiritism obviously tends to revive beliefs founded on the extraordinary and supernatural. However, in our positivistic century, this seems to me to be a problem because it acknowledges popular superstitions and errors that reason has condemned.

A.K. – An idea is superstitious only because it is erroneous; it ceases to be superstitious the moment it is a recognized truth. The issue, therefore, is to know whether there are spirit manifestations or not. Now, you cannot brand something as superstitious until it can be *proven* that it does not, in fact, exist. You will say: my reason refuses to accept such manifestations. Nevertheless, those who do believe in them – and who can hardly be regarded as fools – also call upon their reason in addition to the phenomena; so, which side should you take? The great judge in the matter is the future, just as it has been with all scientific and industrial subjects that were at first branded as absurd and impossible. You judge *a priori* according to your own opinion; we judge only after having taken a long time to watch and observe. We would add that, as enlightened as it is today, Spiritism, on the contrary, tends to destroy superstitious ideas because it shows what is true or erroneous in popular beliefs; everything that is absurd about it has been added out of ignorance and bias.

I would go even further and say that the positivism of our century is precisely what led us to accept Spiritism, and that it partly owes its rapid spread to positivism, and not, as some claim, to a return to the love for the extraordinary and supernatural. The supernatural disappears when exposed to the light of science, philosophy and reason, just as the gods of paganism vanished before the light of Christianity.

The supernatural lies outside the scope of the laws of nature; positivism, on the other hand, accepts nothing outside such laws. But does it know all of them? Throughout time, phenomena whose causes were unknown have been regarded as supernatural; each new law discovered by science, however, has diminished the borders of the supernatural. Well then! Spiritism has come to reveal a new law according to which conversing with the spirit of a deceased person rests upon a law that is as natural as the one that enabled electricity to establish contact between two individuals hundreds of miles apart. The same applies to all the other Spiritist phenomena. As far as Spiritism is concerned, it repudiates every extraordinary effect, i.e., those outside the laws of nature. It performs neither miracles nor prodigies; rather, by virtue of a law, it explains certain effects that have until now been reputed as miracles and prodigies, and as such demonstrates their possibility. Thus, it has broadened the realm of science, and in doing so, it has become a science itself. However, because the discovery of this new law has entailed moral consequences, the codification of such consequences makes it, at the same time, a philosophical doctrine.

From the philosophical point of view, Spiritism responds to people's aspirations concerning the future because it is positive and rational, and that is why it is suitable for the positivist character of the century. You'll understand all this once you put forth the effort to study it.[20]

The Opposition of Science

Visitor – You say you are supported by facts, but you are opposed by the opinion of learned individuals who either contest them or who explain them differently than you. Why didn't they

---

[20] *The Mediums' Book*, chap. II; *Revue Spirite*, Dec. 1861, p. 393, and Jan. 1862, p. 21. Also, see below, chap. II. – Auth.

focus on the turning tables phenomenon? If they had seen anything serious about it, it seems to me that they would not have neglected such extraordinary occurrences, nor would they have rejected them with disdain; however, they are all against you. Aren't learned individuals the guiding light of the nations, and isn't it their duty to spread the light? Why do you suppose they have stifled it when given such a fine opportunity to present to the world the existence of a new force?

A.K. – You have just described the duty of learned individuals quite admirably, and it's unfortunate that they have neglected it on more than one occasion. But before responding to your judicious observation, I must inform you that you are gravely mistaken by saying that all learned individuals are against us.

As I stated just a while ago, it is precisely among the enlightened classes in all the countries of the world that Spiritism has won the most converts. Among them there are a large number of physicians from every nation, and as we know, physicians are men and women of science; the judges, professors, artists, writers, officials, high-ranking public servants, major dignitaries, ecclesiastics, etc. who have gathered under its banner are all persons whom we would not deny as possessing a certain dose of enlightenment. Learned persons are not only to be found within official science and within established organizations.

Because Spiritism doesn't yet have the right to citizenship in official science, is that a reason to condemn it? If science had never been mistaken, its opinion would carry weight in this case; unfortunately, experience has shown otherwise. Hasn't science rejected as pipe dreams a multitude of discoveries that later glorified the memories of their authors? Isn't it due to a report by our elite corps of scholars that France was deprived of the steam power enterprise? When Fulton came to the field at Bologna to present his theory to Napoleon I, who then recommended its immediate examination to the Institute, didn't the Institute conclude that such a theory was an *impractical dream* and that it didn't have the time to bother with it? From this should we conclude that the members of the Institute are unlearned? Does it justify the coarse and tasteless epithets that certain persons enjoy heaping on them? Of course not. There isn't one sensible person who doesn't praise their eminent knowledge, while realizing that they are not infallible and that their judgment is not final, especially when it comes to new ideas.

Visitor – I will be the first to admit that they are not infallible; but it is no less true that, in virtue of their knowledge, their opinion is worth something, and that if you had them on your side, it would give a lot of weight to your theory.

A.K. – But you must also admit that you are only a good judge within your area of competence. If you wanted to build a house, would you employ a musician? If you were ill, would you let yourself be treated by an architect? And if you wanted to file a lawsuit, would you consult a dancer? Lastly, if you had a theological question, would you go to a chemist or an astronomer for an answer? No. To each their own specialty. The regular sciences rest upon the properties of matter, which can be manipulated at will; the phenomena that it produces have material forces as their agents. The phenomena of Spiritism have as their agents intelligent beings, endowed with independence and free will and not subject to our whims; they are not bound by our laboratory procedures or calculations, and are not, therefore, within the scope of science per se.

Science was thus mistaken when it wanted to experiment with spirits the same way it did with a voltaic battery[21]. It failed – as it well should have – because it proceeded based on an analogy that doesn't exist. And then, without going any further, its conclusions were negative. It was a rash judgment, which time has been

---

[21] An electric battery composed of a primary cell or cells. *The American Heritage Dictionary.* – Tr.

rectifying day by day, just as it has done with many others. Those who judged it hastily will be ashamed at having so thoughtlessly set themselves against the infinite power of the Creator.

The scientific community cannot, and never will be able to make a statement on this issue; it is as much outside of their area of competence as it is for them to say whether or not God exists; thus, it is an error to accept their judgment. Spiritism is a matter of personal belief that cannot depend on the vote of an assembly, because such a vote, even if favorable, cannot force conviction. Once public opinion is formed on the matter, scholars will accept it as individuals and submit to the force of things. Let this generation pass, and with it the prejudices of its obstinate self-centeredness and you will see that what happens with Spiritism will be no different from what has happened to so many other contested truths that one would be foolish to question nowadays. Today, believers are the ones who are being called mad; tomorrow, it will be the turn of those who do not believe, just as those who believed the earth spun on its axis used to be called crazy.

Not all learned individuals have judged Spiritism in the same way, however, and by learned individuals I mean individuals of study and knowledge, with or without an official degree. Many have made the following argument:

"There is no effect without a cause, and the most ordinary effects may lead the way to the most difficult problems. If Newton had disregarded the fall of an apple, if Galvani had dismissed his servant as a lunatic and dreamer when he told him about the frogs that danced on the plate, perhaps we still would not have discovered the wonderful law of universal gravity and the numerous properties of the electric battery. The phenomenon sarcastically labeled as the "dance of the tables" is no more ridiculous than the "dance of the frogs", and it too perhaps contains one of those secrets of nature that will revolutionize humankind once it possesses the key."

These learned individuals have stated further: "Since so many people are occupied with spirit phenomena, and since trustworthy individuals have studied them, then there must be something to them after all. An illusion – if you will – cannot have this character of generality; it might bewitch a certain circle or faction, but not the whole world. So let's guard against denying the possibility of what we do not understand, dreading to be proven wrong sooner or later, which would not be very flattering to our judiciousness."

Visitor – Very well, we are talking about a learned individual who reasons with wisdom and prudence; and although I'm not a learned individual myself, I agree with him. Notice, however, that he affirms nothing: he doubts. Thus, on what, exactly, are we to base the belief in the existence of spirits, and especially, the possibility of communicating with them?

A.K. – This belief is based on both reasoning and the facts. I myself did not adopt it until after careful examination. My study of the exact sciences gave me the habit of positivist thinking, which requires thought and analysis, and I probed and scrutinized this new science in its innermost details. I wanted to account for everything because I do not accept an idea before I know the whys and hows. Here is the reasoning I got from an erudite physician who used to be a disbeliever but who is now a fervent adherent:

"It is said that invisible beings communicate; and why not? Before the invention of the microscope, did we suspect the existence of the billions of microscopic organisms that cause such harm to the body? Why is it materially impossible for there to be beings in space that escape our senses? Would we perchance harbor the foolish pretense of knowing everything and tell God that he has nothing more to teach us? If these invisible beings surrounding us are intelligent, why couldn't they communicate with us? If they are in any way related to human beings, they must perform a role in destiny and life's events. Who knows? Maybe it is one of the forces of nature, one of those hidden forces that we never even suspected. What a new horizon this would open up to our thought! What a vast field of observation! The discovery of the world of invisible beings would be much different than the world of the infinitely small; it would be more than a discovery – it would be a revolution in our way of thinking. How much light could be shed! How many mysteries explained! Those who believe in it are ridiculed, but what does that prove? Hasn't it been the same with all great discoveries? Wasn't Christopher Columbus rebuffed, met with disgust and treated as insane? These ideas, it is said, are so strange that no one can believe in them. But anyone who would have said only a half century ago that we would be able to correspond from one part of the world to another in only a few minutes; that we could cross France in just a few hours; that with the steam produced by a little boiling water a ship could go forward against the wind; that we could derive from water the means of providing ourselves with light and warmth; that it would be possible to illuminate all of Paris in an instant with only a reservoir of an invisible substance – surely such a person would have been laughed at. Well then, would it be so utterly exceptional for space to be populated by thinking beings, who, after having lived on the earth, left their material envelopes behind? Don't we find in this fact the explanation of a multitude of beliefs that may be traced back to remotest antiquity? Such matters are well worth delving into."

Such are the thoughts of a learned individual, but an unpretentious one. They are also the thoughts of a huge number of enlightened persons who have understood, not superficially and narrowly, but who, after having examined the matter seriously and without any preconceptions, have had the modesty not to say: I do not understand it; therefore, it does not exist. Their convictions were formed by observation and reasoning. If these ideas were a passing fancy, do you think that such an intellectual elite would have adopted them? That they could have been victims of an illusion for so long?

Hence, it is not materially impossible for there to be beings invisible to us populating space, and this consideration alone should lead to more circumspection. A short time ago, who would have thought that a drop of clear water could contain thousands of beings so small that it would boggle our minds? I would say that it was much harder for our minds to conceive of such subtle beings, having all our organs and functioning like us, than to believe in the beings that we call *spirits*.

Visitor – Of course, but just because something might be possible doesn't mean that it actually exists.

A.K. – I agree, but you must concur that, the moment it ceases to be impossible, that is an important start because it is no longer repugnant to reason. All that remains is to verify it by observing the facts. This is nothing new: sacred and secular history have both demonstrated the ancientness and universality of this belief, which has continued through all the unexpected changes in the world, and which can be found among the most primitive peoples in the form of innate and intuitive ideas engraved on their minds like the belief in the Supreme Being and the future existence. Spiritism, therefore, is not a modern creation – far from it; everything proves that the ancients knew about it as well as we do and perhaps even better, except that it was taught only with mysterious precautions that rendered it inaccessible to the common folk, who were intentionally left in the quagmire of superstition.

As for the phenomena, they are of two natures: some are spontaneous and some are induced. Among the spontaneous phenomena, we list the highly common visions and apparitions, in addition to noises, raps or movements of objects without apparent physical cause. Also listed are a large number of unusual effects that used to be regarded as supernatural, but which nowadays seem so common to us that we find nothing supernatural about them since they all belong to the realm of the immutable laws of nature. As for induced phenomena, they are the ones that are obtained through mediums.

Erroneous Explanations of the Phenomena

Hallucination. – Magnetic fluid. – Thought reflection. – Overexcitement of the brain. – The somnambulistic state of mediums.

Visitor – Criticism has been mostly aimed at the induced phenomena. Let's put aside any supposition of charlatanism and base it on good faith; mightn't we think that mediums are pawns of a hallucination?

A.K. – I don't know if the mechanism of hallucination has yet been explained clearly. As it is understood, it is a most singular effect and well worth studying. So why is it that those who try to explain spirit phenomena based on this premise cannot explain their own explanation? Furthermore, there are phenomena that rule out this hypothesis: when a table or other object moves, rises or raps; when it moves at will around a room without coming in contact with anyone; when it rises up from the floor and remains suspended in the air without any point of support; and lastly, when it collapses and crashes to the floor – this is certainly not a hallucination. Supposing that, through an effect of their imagination, mediums believe they are seeing something that does not actually exist, is it possible that an entire community could be caught up in the same figment of the imagination? That it would be repeated far and wide, in every land? The hallucination in that case would be more prodigious than the phenomenon itself.

Visitor – If we were to accept the reality of the turning and rapping table phenomenon, wouldn't it be more rational to attribute it to the action of some fluid – the magnetic fluid, for example?

A.K. – That was actually my first thought, and that of many others. If the effects had been limited to material effects, there is no doubt that we could have explained them in that way. However, when the movements and raps gave proof of intelligence and when it was realized that they responded to thought with complete freedom, we had to draw the following conclusion: *If every effect has a cause, then every intelligent effect has an intelligent cause.* If it were the effect of a fluid, wouldn't we have to say that the fluid was intelligent? When we see the arm of a telegraph make the signals that transmit thought, we know very well that it is not the wooden or iron arm that is intelligent, but we say that an intelligence is making them move. The same happens with the table. Are there or aren't there intelligent effects? That is the question. Those who contest it are persons who didn't see the whole picture and rushed to draw conclusions according to their own ideas and a superficial observation.

Visitor – I would respond to that by saying that if there is an intelligent effect, it comes from nothing more than intelligence itself, whether of the medium, the questioner or one of the participants, because it is said that the response is always within someone's thought.

A.K. – That is yet another error following a faulty observation. If those who think that way had put forth the effort to study the phenomenon in all its aspects, they would have recognized at each step the complete independence of the manifesting intelligences. How can this theory be reconciled with responses that are outside the intellectual capacity and education of the mediums, that are contrary to their own ideas, desires and opinions, or that completely baffle the expectations of the onlookers? What about mediums writing in a language unknown to them or in their own language when they don't even know how to read or write? I will admit that at first sight this theory has nothing irrational about it, but it is contradicted by facts so numerous and so conclusive that doubt is no longer possible.

Furthermore, even if we were to accept this theory, the phenomenon, far from being simplified, would then, in fact, be quite extraordinary. Imagine! Could thought actually be reflected on surfaces like light, sound or heat? That would truly be something that would stoke science's interest. Also, what would make it even more extraordinary is the fact that, out of twenty participants, it would be the thought of this or that particular individual that is reflected rather than the thought of one of the others. Such a theory is unsustainable. It is truly interesting to see opponents do their utmost to find causes a hundred times more extraordinary and difficult to understand than the ones that are offered to them.

Visitor – According to the opinion of some, couldn't we say that mediums in such cases are in an altered state and are enjoying a lucidity that gives them a somnambulistic perception, a sort of second sight? That would explain the momentary broadening of their intellectual faculties, since it is said that the communications obtained by mediums do not exceed the scope of those obtained by somnambulists.

A.K. – That is yet another theory that doesn't hold up under serious examination. These mediums are not in an altered state, nor are they asleep; they are wide awake, acting and thinking like everyone else, displaying nothing out of the ordinary. Certain particular effects might have given rise to this mistake. However, those who do not limit their judgment to only one angle would easily realize that mediums are endowed with a unique faculty that does not allow confusing them with somnambulists, and that the complete independence of their thought is proven by facts of indisputable evidence. Written communications aside, what somnambulist has ever made an inert body produce a thought? Or produced visible and even tangible apparitions? Or kept a heavy object suspended in the air with no point of support? Was it by some somnambulistic effect that a medium once drew for me, in the presence of twenty witnesses, the portrait of a young woman who had died eighteen months earlier, and whom he had never known, but whose father at the session recognized her? Is it due to a somnambulistic effect that a table accurately answers questions put to it – even those posed only mentally? Even if we were to actually believe the medium is in a magnetic state, it would still seem hard to believe that the table is somnambulistic.

It is also said that mediums speak intelligibly only about things that are known. Then how can the following occurrence and a hundred others like it be explained? One of my friends, a very good writing medium, asked a spirit if a person he had not seen for fifteen years was still in this world. "Yes, she is still alive," it answered; "she lives in Paris, on such and such a street, at such and such a number." He went and found the person at the address indicated. Is that an illusion? His thought could hardly have suggested the response, since considering the person's age, there was every possibility that she was no longer even alive. If in certain cases answers have actually matched thoughts, is it rational to conclude that it is a general law? In this, as in all matters, hasty judgments are always dangerous because they can be invalidated by facts that have not been looked at.

Disbelievers Cannot See in order to be Convinced

Visitor – It is actual phenomena that disbelievers would like to see, that they ask for, and that most of the time they cannot be furnished with. If people could witness these occurrences, there would be no more room for doubt. How is it, then, that so many people haven't been allowed to see anything in spite of their willingness? One might argue that it is due to their lack of faith, but to that they correctly reply that they cannot have faith in advance, and that if belief is desired of them, they must be given the means to believe.

A.K. – The reason is quite simple. They want the phenomena to happen at their command, but spirits do not obey commands; one must wait for their good will. Hence, it isn't enough to say: Show me this or that phenomenon and I will believe; one must have the willingness to persevere, to let the phenomena occur spontaneously, without trying to force or direct them. The ones that are hoped for will perhaps be exactly the ones that are not received. But others will appear, and the one hoped for will come at a time when it is least expected. To the eyes of the attentive and diligent observer, they will appear collectively, corroborating each other. However, those who think that it is enough to turn a crank to start the machine are badly mistaken. What do naturalists do when they want to study the habits of animals? Do they command them to do such and such a thing so they may have the leisure to observe them as they please? No, because they know very well that the subject will not obey them; they *watch for* spontaneous expressions of their instinct; they wait and learn about them as they occur. Plain common sense shows that it is even more reasonable that the same would apply to spirits, who are intelligences much more independent than animals.

It is wrong to believe that faith is necessary, but *good faith* – that is something different. There are skeptics who deny the evidence, and not even miracles could convince them. How many are there who, having seen the phenomena, nonetheless insist on explaining them in their own way, saying that it doesn't prove anything! Such people serve only to disrupt meetings without any benefit to themselves. That is why we should avoid them and not want to waste any time on them. There are those who would become downright angry at being forced to believe, because their pride would suffer at having to admit that they were wrong. What can we say to people who see nothing but illusion and charlatanism everywhere? Nothing; we must leave them alone and say, as is their desire, that they did, in fact, see nothing, and even say that no one was able or willing to enable them to see.

Alongside these hardened skeptics there are those who want to see things their own way; who, having formed an opinion, want everything to relate to it. They do not understand that the phenomena will not obey their will; they do not know how to – or do not want to – situate themselves in the necessary conditions. Those who want to observe in good faith should not believe without question, but rid themselves of all preconceived ideas and not want to compare incompatible things. They should wait, follow and observe with tireless patience. The same applies to adherents, since it shows that they haven't arrived at their convictions lightly. Do you have such patience? No, you will say; I don't have the time. Then don't concern yourself with it; but don't talk about it either – no one is making you.

Spirits' Good or Ill Will to Convince

Visitor – All that being said, it seems that spirits ought to be interested in making converts. Why don't they lend themselves more than they do to ways that would convince certain individuals whose opinion would have a great influence?

A.K. – Because apparently, for now, they aren't interested in convincing certain individuals whose importance they do not consider to be as great as such individuals think it is. I will admit that this is not very flattering, but we cannot control their opinions; spirits have a way of judging things that is not always like our own. They see, think and act according to other perspectives; whereas our sight is circumscribed by matter, limited by the narrow circle in which we find ourselves, spirits embrace the whole. Time, which seems so long to us, is only an instant for them; distance is only a step; certain details that may seem extremely important to us are childish to them; on the other hand, they deem as important certain things whose significance we do not grasp. In order to understand them, we must raise ourselves in thought above our material and mental horizon and see things from their perspective. It isn't for them to come down to us, but for us to go up to them, and that is done through study and observation.

Spirits appreciate diligent and conscientious observers, and they multiply the sources of enlightenment for them. What keeps them away is not doubt born of ignorance, but the self-complacency of supposed observers who observe nothing, who intend only to put them in the spotlight and manipulate them like puppets while harboring a sentiment of hostility and disparagement whether in thoughts or in words. Spirits do nothing for these and are very little concerned about what they might say or think, because their time will come. That is why I have said that it is not faith per se that is necessary, but good faith.

The Origin of Modern Spiritist Ideas

Visitor – One thing I would like to know, sir, is the origin of modern Spiritist ideas. Are they really a spontaneous revelation by the spirits or are they the result of a prior belief in their existence? You can understand the importance of my question because in the latter case, one could believe that imagination might have played a role.

A.K. – As you have put it, this question is important for such a point of view, although it is difficult to believe – assuming that Spiritist ideas were born of a prior belief – that the imagination could have produced all the material results that have been observed. In fact, if Spiritism had been founded on the preconceived thought of the existence of spirits, one could, with some semblance of reason, doubt their reality, for if a cause is merely a pipe dream, the consequences themselves must be imaginary; however, things do not happen like that.

Note first that this line of reasoning is completely illogical. Spirits are a cause and not an effect; when we see an effect, we can look for the cause, but it is not natural to imagine a cause *before having seen the effects*. Thus, we couldn't conceive the idea of spirits unless there were effects that might be explained by the existence of invisible beings. Well, that is not the way the idea appeared; that is, it was not a hypothesis imagined in order to explain certain phenomena; the first supposition made about them was one of an entirely material cause. Thus, rather than spirits having been a preconceived idea, we started from a *materialistic* point of view. And since this point of view was unable to explain everything, observation alone led to the spirit-related cause. I speak of modern Spiritist ideas since we know that the belief in spirits is as old as the world itself. This is how the matter progressed:

Spontaneous phenomena, such as strange noises, raps, movements of objects, etc., were produced without an ostensible cause and under the influence of certain persons. Up to this point, nothing had warranted looking for a cause other than the action of a magnetic or other fluid whose properties were still unknown. But it didn't take long to recognize an intentional and intelligent character in these noises and movements, from which it was deduced, as I have already stated, that if every effect has a cause, every intelligent effect must have an intelligent cause. This intelligence could not have resided in the object itself, because matter is not intelligent. Was it the reflection of the intelligence of the person or persons present? That is what was initially thought, as I have also stated. Experience alone could pronounce itself on the matter, and on many occasions, experience demonstrated, through irrefutable proofs, the complete independence of this intelligence. Thus, it had to be outside the object and outside the person. But what was it? The intelligence itself answered this question, stating that it belonged to the order of incorporeal beings called *spirits*. So, the idea of spirits was not *a priori*, nor was it even *a posteriori*; in other words, it did not come from the mind but was given by the spirits themselves, and everything we have learned about them ever since has been taught to us by the spirits themselves.

Once the existence of spirits was revealed and the means of communicating with them established, we were able to have continual conversations with them and to obtain information about their nature, the conditions of their existence and their role in the visible world. If we could interrogate the beings from the world of the infinitesimal in the same way, how many interesting things we could learn about them!

If we were to suppose that, before the discovery of America, there had been an electric wire stretched across the Atlantic, and that signs of intelligence were received at its European end, we would have concluded that there were intelligent beings at the other end wanting to communicate; they could have been questioned and they would have answered. Thus, we would have acquired certainty of their existence, knowledge of their customs, their habits and way of living without having ever seen them. It was the same with the relations with the invisible world: the physical manifestations were like signals, a means of awareness that put us on the path to more regular and continuous communications. And remarkably, as easier means of communication became available, the spirits abandoned the primitive, insufficient and cumbersome means, just as the speech-impaired would give up sign language if they recovered their ability to speak.

Who were the inhabitants of this world? Were they separate beings outside of humanity? Were they good or evil? Once again, experimentation was entrusted with resolving these questions. But until numerous observations had thrown light on the subject, the field of conjectures and theories was wide open, and God knows how many appeared! Some believed spirits were superior in every way, whereas others saw them only as demons. It was by their own words and actions, however, that we were able to tell what they were. Let's suppose that, regarding the unknown transatlantic inhabitants we have just mentioned, some said good things, whereas others were noticed for the cynicism of their speech. This would lead us to conclude that there were good and bad ones. The same happened in the case of spirits: it was through a similar process that we discerned every degree of goodness and wickedness, ignorance and knowledge among them. Once enlightened about their faults and qualities, it fell to our own judiciousness to distinguish the good from the evil, the true from the false in their relations with us – exactly as we do with regards to humans.

Observation enlightened us not only about the moral qualities of spirits but also their nature and what we might call their physiological state. We learned from the spirits themselves that some are very happy and others very unhappy; that they are not separate beings of an exceptional nature, but the souls of those who used to live on the earth, where they had left their corporeal envelope behind; that they inhabit space, surround us and continually rub elbows with us; that, through indisputable signs, anyone could recognize among them their *relatives, friends and those whom they knew here on earth*; that they could be followed in all the phases of their existence beyond the grave from the moment they left their bodies, and their situation could be observed according to their kind of death and the manner in which they had lived on the earth. Lastly, it was realized that they are not abstract, incorporeal beings, in the absolute sense of the word. They have an envelope, to which we gave the name *perispirit*, a sort of fluidic, vaporous, diaphanous body that is invisible in the normal state, but which, in certain cases and by a kind of condensation or molecular arrangement, can become momentarily visible and even tangible; hence, the phenomena of apparitions and the ability to touch them were explained. This envelope exists throughout the life of the body; it is the link between the spirit and matter. When the body dies, the soul, or spirit – which is the same thing – casts off only the coarse envelope and keeps the second one, much like when we remove an outer garment and keep only the one beneath, or when the seed of a fruit casts off the cortical envelope and keeps only the *perisperm*. It is this semi-material envelope of the spirit that is the agent of the different phenomena through which it manifests its presence.

Such is the story of Spiritism in a few words; once you have studied it in-depth, you will see and realize even better that everything concerning it is the result of observation and not a preconceived theory.

Means of Communication

Visitor – You mentioned the means of communication; could you give me an idea about them since it is hard to understand how these invisible beings can converse with us?

A.K. – Gladly; I will do so only briefly, however, because it would demand long drawn-out explanations that you can find particularly in *The Mediums' Book*. But the little I will tell you will suffice to set you on the path of the mechanism, and will help you, above all, to better understand some of the sessions you might attend while awaiting your full initiation.

The existence of the semi-material envelope, or perispirit, is a key that explains many things and demonstrates the possibility of certain phenomena. As for the means per se, they are quite varied and depend either on the degree of purity of the spirits themselves or on the particular dispositions of the persons who serve as their intermediaries. The most common one – the one we might call universal – consists of intuition, that is, of the ideas and thoughts they suggest to us; but this method is little considered in most cases. There are others that are more dependable.

Certain spirits communicate by raps, answering either *yes* or *no,* or designating individual letters to form words. These raps may be obtained by spirits tilting an object – a table, for example, that strikes one of its legs on the floor; but quite often, they make themselves heard within the actual material of the object, without the object making any movement at all. This primitive approach is slow and doesn't easily lend itself to communicating lengthier ideas. Writing has replaced it and is obtained in different ways. At first, we used a movable object such as a small planchette, a basket or a box, to which we attached a pencil whose point rested on the paper. We still use this method at times. The nature and substance of the object doesn't matter. The medium places his or her hands on the object, transmitting to it the influence he or she receives from the spirit, and the pencil writes the letters. But properly speaking, this object is nothing more than an extension of the hand, a sort of pencil holder. We have since recognized that it is pointless to use this intermediary object because it merely complicates the process. Its sole merit was that it physically established the mediums' independence, but they can write just as well by holding the pencil themselves.

Spirits can also express themselves by transmitting their thoughts through articulated sounds that either resound in the air or in the ears, as well as through the medium's voice, through sight, drawings, music, and other means that a thorough study would reveal. For these different means, mediums have special aptitudes connected with their physical and mental make-up. Thus we have physical effects mediums, that is, those who are able to produce physical phenomena such as raps, the movement of objects, etc. There are also hearing, speaking, seeing, drawing, musical and writing mediums. This last faculty is the most common, the most easily developed through practice; it is also the most valuable because it allows for the most regular and the quickest communications.

There are several kinds of writing mediums, two of which are very distinct. In order to understand them, we must understand how the phenomenon occurs. The spirit sometimes acts directly on the medium's hand, to which it gives an impulse that is completely independent of the medium's will. The medium has no awareness of what is being written: this is the *mechanical medium*. In other cases, the spirit acts on the brain; its thought passes through that of the medium. Although the medium writes involuntarily, he or she is more or less clearly aware of what is being received: this is the *intuitive medium*. The medium's role is exactly like that of interpreters who transmit a thought that is not their own, although they do understand it. Although in this case the spirit's thought and that of the medium sometimes intermingle, experience has taught us how to easily distinguish them. Equally good communications may be obtained through both these types of mediums; the advantage of the mechanical type is that it is particularly effective on people who are not yet convinced. Besides, the essential qualities of mediums are to be found much more in the nature of the spirits who assist them and in the communications they receive than in the means by which the communications are received.

Visitor – The procedure seems simple enough. Would it be possible for me to try it out myself?

A.K. – Certainly; I would even say that if you have been endowed with this mediumistic faculty, it would be the best way to convince you because you couldn't doubt your own good faith. But I would strongly urge you not to try it out before having studied it carefully. Communications from beyond the grave are fraught with more difficulties than one might think; they are not exempt from pitfalls or even dangers for those who lack the necessary experience. It is like someone who would like to experiment with chemicals without knowing chemistry: the person could run the risk of burning his or her fingers.

Visitor – Is there any sign by which one can recognize this aptitude?

A.K. – So far, we don't know of any diagnoses for mediumship; those we thought we had identified turned out to be worthless. Experimentation is the only way to know if one is endowed with the faculty. Moreover, mediums are very numerous, and if we ourselves are not mediums, it is extremely rare for us not to find one amongst our family members or the persons with whom we associate. Sex, age and temperament don't matter; men and women, children and the elderly, as well as individuals who are well and those who are sick may be mediums.

If mediumship were conveyed by some outward sign, this would imply that the faculty is permanent, whereas it is essentially changeable and temporary. Its physical cause lies in how easily the perispiritual fluids of the incarnate and discarnate spirit are assimilated. Its moral cause lies in the will of the spirit, who communicates when it wants to, and not in our own will. From this we may conclude that, first, not all spirits can communicate indiscriminately through all mediums, and that, second, all mediums are capable of losing or having their faculty suspended when they least expect it. This brief summary should be enough to show you that there is a great deal of study to be done in order to recognize the variations that this phenomenon presents.

Thus, it would be a mistake to think that any spirit whatsoever can come when called and communicate through the first medium at hand. For a spirit to communicate, first, it must agree to do so; second, its position or activities must allow it to; and third, it must find the medium to be a suitable instrument, adequate to its nature.

In principle, one may communicate with spirits of all orders, with relatives and friends, with the most highly evolved spirits as well as with the commonest; apart from possible individual situations, however, they come more willingly or less so according to the circumstances, and *especially* according to their affinity for the persons who call them, and not because of the request of the first person who, on a whim, evokes them out of curiosity. In such a case they would not have bothered with it when alive, much less after death.

Serious spirits come only to serious meetings, where they are called in an atmosphere of *respect and for serious reasons*; they pay no heed to any questions of curiosity or proof, useless purpose or experimentation.

Frivolous spirits go everywhere, but at serious meetings they remain quiet and stand aside to listen, like students at a gathering of scholars. They have fun at frivolous meetings, however, where they are amused by everything, frequently mock those in attendance, and answer everything with no concern for the truth.

Spirits known as rapping spirits, and in general, all those who produce physical manifestations, are of a lower order, although they are not necessarily evil because of it; they simply have a somewhat special aptitude for physical effects. High order spirits do not concern themselves with such things any more than scholars concern themselves with feats of strength; if high order spirits need to communicate through physical means, they use these spirits, just as we use laborers for heavier work.

Mediums for Hire

Visitor – Before they delve into a prolonged course of study, some people would like to be certain that they will not be wasting their time, and certain that they will be provided with a conclusive fact, even if they have to pay for it.

A.K. – People who don't want to go to the trouble of studying display more curiosity than an actual desire to learn. Well, spirits don't like the curious any more than I do. Moreover, cupidity is especially disagreeable to them, and they don't lend themselves to anything that may satisfy it. One would have to have a very wrong idea of them to believe that highly evolved spirits such as Fenelon, Bossuet, Pascal or St. Augustine would submit to the orders of the first person who showed up and paid a certain amount per hour. No, sir; communications from beyond the grave are too serious and require too much respect to serve as exhibitions.

Moreover, we know that spirit phenomena do not function like the gears of some mechanism, because they depend on the will of the spirits. Even if a person does have a mediumistic faculty, he or she cannot claim to be able to obtain spirit phenomena at any given moment. If disbelievers are inclined to suspect the good faith of mediums in general, it would be much worse if mediums harbored a desire of profit. They would have good reason to suspect that paid mediums would simulate the phenomena when spirits were not actually present because their main concern would be getting paid. Not only is absolute disinterest the best guarantee of authenticity, it would be repugnant to our reason to ask the spirits of our loved ones to come for a price – even supposing they would consent to it, which is more than doubtful. In any case, it would involve only low order spirits who were unscrupulous as to the means and undeserving of any trust. Furthermore, such spirits often take malicious pleasure in foiling the schemes and calculations of those who try to control them at will.

The nature of the mediumistic faculty is thus opposed to its becoming a profession, since the faculty depends on a will foreign to the medium; and it can fail to manifest at the moment the medium needs it most, unless he or she can supply it with skilful dexterity. But even admitting complete good faith, since phenomena cannot be obtained at will, it would be by sheer chance if during a paid session a phenomenon were produced because of a desire to be convinced. We could give a hundred thousand francs to a medium and we wouldn't enable him or her to get the spirits to do what they didn't want to do. This enticement not only distorts the intention and transforms it into an intense desire for profit, but quite to the contrary, it is a reason for the medium not to be successful. If we are well imbued with this truth, that is, that affection and affinity are the most powerful incentives for attracting spirits, we will understand that they cannot be solicited with the thought of being used to make money.

Therefore, those who need phenomena to be convinced should prove their goodwill to the spirits by means of serious and patient observation if they want to be assisted by them. But if it is true that faith cannot be imposed, it is no less true that it cannot be bought.

Visitor – I can understand this line of reasoning from a moral point of view; however, isn't it fair for those who give their time to the interest of their cause to be compensated for it if it keeps them from working for a living?

A. K. – In the first place, are they really doing it in the interest of their cause, or are they doing it for their own gain? If they did leave their job, it was because they were not satisfied with it, and because they hope to earn more or work less at their new one. There is no self-sacrifice in giving one's time when it can lead to making a profit from it. That would be like saying that the baker makes bread in the interest of humankind. Mediumship isn't the only resource open to them; without it, they would have to earn their living some other way. When they do not have independent means, truly serious and devoted mediums look for ways to earn a living with regular work, and they do not give up their jobs. They devote only as much time as they can to their mediumship without jeopardizing themselves, and if they do so voluntarily in their leisure time or rest, it is simply devotion on their part; they are thus valued and respected all the more for it.

Furthermore, the large number of family mediums makes professional mediums unnecessary, even supposing that they offer all the desirable guarantees, a fact that is extremely rare. Without the discredit that is attributed to this kind of exploitation – a discredit I am happy to have contributed to extensively – we would have seen mediums for hire multiply and newspapers covered with their advertisements. For each honest medium, there would have been a hundred charlatans who, by exploiting an authentic or *simulated* faculty, would have done great harm to Spiritism. It is therefore a given that all those who see in Spiritism something beyond an exhibition of curious phenomena, and who understand and value the dignity, consideration and genuine interests of the doctrine, condemn every type of speculation in whatever form or *disguise* it presents itself. Serious and sincere mediums – and I give this name to those who understand the sanctity of the mandate that God has entrusted to them – avoid even the appearance of what might suggest the slightest hint of cupidity casting its shadow over them. The accusation of making any profit with their faculty would be regarded by them as an insult.

Complete disbeliever that you are, you must admit, sir, that mediums with such conduct would make an entirely different impression on you than if you had paid for your seat to see them operate, or, in the event you had been given free admission, if you knew that behind it the purpose was money. You must admit that if you saw mediums animated by a true religious sentiment, stimulated only by faith and not by the desire for profit, they would unwittingly command your respect, even if they were from the humblest working class. They would inspire you with more trust because you would have no reason to doubt their honesty. Well, sir, you can find thousands of them, and it is one of the causes that have contributed powerfully to the credit and spread of the doctrine, whereas if it had had only interpreters interested in making a profit, it would not have a quarter of the adherents it has today.

It is well-known that professional mediums are extremely rare, at least in France; that they are unknown in most of the Spiritist centers in the country, where a reputation as mediums for hire would be enough for them to be excluded from any serious group. Furthermore, the job would not be very profitable for them due to the discredit they would cause and the competition of disinterested mediums, who may be found everywhere. To make up for it, whether it is the mediumistic faculty they lack or a shortage of clientele, there are the so-called mediums who use card games, egg whites, coffee grounds, etc., to satisfy every taste, hoping in this way and in the absence of spirits, to attract those who still believe in such foolishness. If they harmed only themselves, the evil would be minor; but there are individuals who, without going any farther, mistake the abuse for the reality, and then the ill-intentioned take advantage of it by saying that that is what Spiritism is all about. So you can see that when the exploitation of mediumship leads to abuses that jeopardize the doctrine, serious Spiritism is right in condemning it and repudiating it as an aid.

Visitor – All that is very logical, I must agree, but non-paid mediums are not at just anybody's disposal; furthermore, it would not be right to bother them, whereas there would be no problem with going to someone who gets paid because it wouldn't make them waste their time. If there were *public mediums*, it would make it easier for people who wanted to be convinced.

A.K. – But if public mediums – as you call them – could not offer any guarantees, of what use could they be for convincing anyone? The drawback you have indicated doesn't cancel out the other, more serious ones that I have mentioned. People would go to public mediums more for the sheer amusement of it or to have their fortunes told than to get enlightenment. Those who seriously wish to be convinced will find the means sooner or later if they have perseverance and goodwill; however, they won't be convinced by attending a session if they haven't been prepared for it. If they take an unfavorable impression with them, they will leave even less convinced than before, and will perhaps put off the idea of pursuing the study of something in which they saw nothing serious; experience has proven this.

But aside from the moral considerations, the progress of today's Spiritist science has shown us a material difficulty that we did not suspect in the beginning, but which has made us more aware of the conditions in which manifestations are produced. This problem has to do with the fluidic affinities that must exist between the evoked spirit and the medium.

I put aside any thought of fraud and deception, and I presume complete honesty. In order for professional mediums to elicit full trust from the people who consult them, they would have to possess a permanent and universal faculty; that is, they would have to be able to communicate easily with any spirit and at any given moment; like doctors, they would have to be constantly at the public's disposal, and they would have to satisfy any evocation that might be asked of them. However, paid or not, mediums cannot offer such guarantees due to causes independent of the spirit's will, which I will not describe in-depth, because I am not giving you a course in Spiritism. I will limit myself to saying that fluidic affinities, which are the very basis for the mediumistic faculties, are *individual* and not *general*, and that the medium might have them regarding one particular spirit but not another; that without these affinities, whose nuances are very numerous, communications are incomplete, erroneous or impossible; that most frequently, the fluidic assimilation between the spirit and the medium is established only over time, and only in *one case out of ten* is it established the very first time. So, as you can see, sir, mediumship is subject to laws that are in some way organic, and to which every medium is subject. Thus, you cannot deny that this would be an obstacle to professional mediumship, since the potential for precise communications is linked to causes independent of both the medium and the spirit. (See below, chap. II, sect. *Concerning Mediums*).

Therefore, if we reject the exploitation of mediumship, it is not because of caprice or principle, but because the very tenets that govern communications with the invisible world are opposed to the regularity and precision that would be required for those who would place themselves at the public's disposal, and because the desire to satisfy a paying clientele would lead to abuse. I would not conclude from all this that all mediums for hire are charlatans, but I would say that the interest in making a profit encourages charlatanism and at least warrants suspicion of fraud if it does not justify it outright. Those who wish to be convinced should, more than anything else, look for the elements of authenticity.

Mediums and Sorcerers

Visitor – Since mediumship consists in communicating with unseen powers, it seems to me that mediums and sorcerers are almost the same thing.

A.K. – In every age there have been natural, unconscious mediums who, just because they produced unusual and misunderstood phenomena, were labeled as sorcerers and were accused of making a pact with the Devil. It was the same with most of the learned individuals who possessed knowledge beyond the ordinary. Ignorance increased their power, and they themselves often abused public credulity by exploiting it; hence their justified condemnation. We only need compare the power attributed to sorcerers with the faculty of genuine mediums to see the difference, but most critics do not go to the trouble. Far from reviving sorcery, Spiritism has destroyed it forever by stripping it of its supposed supernatural power, formulas, conjuring books, amulets and talismans, and by reducing the feasible phenomena to their rightful worth, without departing from natural laws.

The similarity that certain people claim exists comes from their error in thinking that *spirits are under mediums' orders*; it is repugnant to their reason to believe that the first medium to come along could make the spirit of this or that relatively illustrious character respond to the medium's beck and call at just that given moment. They are absolutely right in this, and if they had taken the trouble to familiarize themselves with Spiritism before casting stones at it, they would know it states very clearly that *spirits are not at the command of anyone's whim, and no one can make them come at will and against their wishes*; from which it follows that mediums are not sorcerers.

Visitor – Based on this, wouldn't all the effects that certain accredited mediums obtain at will and in public be, according to you, nothing more than trickery?

A. K. – I wouldn't say so categorically. Such phenomena are not impossible, because there are low order spirits who may willingly participate and have fun with these sorts of things, having perhaps been in the sleight-of-hand trade themselves when alive. Moreover, there are mediums especially suited to these kinds of manifestations; nonetheless, the most average common sense rejects the idea that even little-evolved spirits would turn up to put on a show and perform clever feats simply to amuse the curious.

Obtaining these phenomena at will – and especially in public – is always suspect; in this case, mediumship and sleight-of-hand are so similar that it is often very hard to distinguish one from the other. Before seeing the action of spirits in such a situation, meticulous observation is required, either taking into account the medium's character and antecedents or a multitude of circumstances that only a thorough study of the theory of spirit phenomena can enable us to evaluate. It is worth noting that this type of mediumship – when mediumship is actually involved – is limited to producing the same phenomenon over and over with a few variants, which is not likely to clear up any doubts about it. An absolute disinterestedness is the best guarantee of authenticity.

Whatever the reality of these phenomena may be, as mediumistic effects, they have a good result in that they lend impact to the Spiritist idea. The controversy surrounding this subject stimulates many to study the subject more deeply. Of course, it is not there that Spiritism's true teachings or its philosophy should be sought, but it is a way to grab the attention of the indifferent and to force the most recalcitrant to talk about them.

Diversity among Spirits

Visitor – You speak of good or evil, serious or frivolous spirits; I must admit that I do not understand this difference. It seems to me that, upon leaving their corporeal envelope, they must shed the imperfections inherent to matter; that light must shine for them regarding all the truths that are hidden from them, and that they surely must be free of earthly prejudices.

A.K. – Of course they are free of physical imperfections, that is, bodily illnesses and infirmities; however, moral imperfections have to do with the spirit and not the body. Among their numbers are those who are intellectually and morally advanced to varying degrees. It would be a mistake to believe that after having left their material bodies, spirits are suddenly struck with the light of truth. Do you believe, for example, that when you die, there will be no difference between your own spirit and that of a primitive or an evildoer? If that were so, what good would it have done to have worked on your education and improvement since a villain would be just like you after death? Spirits progress only gradually and sometimes very slowly. Some of them – and this depends on their purification – see things from a more correct point of view than during their physical life; on the other hand, others still have the same passions, the same prejudices and the same misapprehensions until time and new trials enable them to enlighten themselves. Be well aware that this is the result of experience because this is the way they present themselves to us in their communications. Hence, it is an elementary principle of Spiritism that there are spirits of all levels of intelligence and morality.

Visitor – But then, why aren't all spirits perfect? What you have said would seem to imply that God has created all sorts of categories.

A.K. – That would be like asking why all the students at a college are not philosophy majors. All spirits have the same origin and the same destiny. The differences among them do not constitute different kinds, but different degrees of advancement.

Spirits are not perfect, because they are the souls of human beings, and humans are not perfect; likewise, humans are not perfect, because they are the incarnation of spirits that are of varying degrees of advancement. The corporeal world and the spirit world are constantly intermingling; through the death of the body, the corporeal world supplies its contingent to the spirit world; through birth, the spirit world supplies humankind. With each new existence, the spirit accomplishes much or little progress, and when it has acquired on earth the full knowledge and moral elevation possible for our globe, it leaves it and goes to a more highly evolved world, where it learns new things.

The spirits who form earth's invisible population are in a way the reflection of the corporeal world; one finds there the same vices and the same virtues. Among them there are the learned, the ignorant, the pseudo-learned, the wise and the foolish, the philosophers, the thinkers, the theorizers. And since they haven't rid themselves of their prejudices, all political and religious factions have their representatives there. They speak according to their own ideas, and what they say is often nothing more than their personal opinion. That is why we must not blindly believe everything spirits say.

Visitor – If that is so, I can see a big problem. In this conflict of diverse opinions, how does one distinguish error from truth? I can't see what good spirits are to us or what we have to gain from communicating with them.

A.K. – If spirits served only to teach us that there are, in fact, spirits and that these spirits are the souls of humans, wouldn't that be of great importance to all those who doubt that they even have a soul, and who do not know what will become of them after death?

As with all philosophical sciences, this one demands lengthy study and meticulous observation in order for us to learn to distinguish the truth from falsehood and to keep deceitful spirits away. Above the throngs of low order spirits, there are high order ones, who have only the good in mind and whose mission is to lead people to the right path. It is up to us to know how to recognize and understand them. They teach us great things, but we mustn't think that studying the others is useless; in order to get to know the inhabitants of a place, we must observe them in all their aspects.

You yourself have proof of this; you thought that it was enough for spirits to leave their corporeal envelope to rid themselves of their imperfections. However, communications with them have taught us just the opposite, and have made us aware of the true state of the spirit world, something which is of a high degree of interest to all of us since we all have to go there. As for the errors that can arise from spirits' differences of opinion, these vanish by themselves once we learn to distinguish between the good and the evil, the learned and the ignorant, the sincere and the hypocritical, exactly as we do amongst ourselves; common sense exposes false doctrines.

Visitor – My observation arises from the point of view of scientific questions and others that we can put to the spirits. The differences in their opinions regarding the theories that divide scholars leave us in doubt. I can understand that since not all of them are knowledgeable to the same degree, they cannot all know everything. But then of what use could the opinions of those who do know be for us if we cannot tell who is right or wrong? It wouldn't matter if we addressed either humans or spirits.

A.K. – That thought is another result of not knowing Spiritism's true character. Those who think they can use it as an easy way to know everything, to discover everything, are greatly mistaken. Spirits are not responsible for bringing us ready-made knowledge. In fact, it would be too convenient if all we had to do was ask in order to be helped, thus sparing us the trouble of doing the research. God wants us to work, to exercise our thought, and we cannot acquire knowledge except at such price. Spirits do not come to exempt us from this necessity; *they are what they are, and the object of Spiritism is to study them* in order to learn by analogy what we will become one day, and not to enable us to know what must remain hidden from us, or to reveal things before the proper time.

Furthermore, spirits can no longer be taken for fortune-tellers, and those who pride themselves on getting certain secrets from them should be prepared for strange deceptions on the part of mocking spirits. In other words, *Spiritism is a science of observation and not a science of divination or speculation.* We study it in order to understand the state of the individual inhabitants of the invisible world, the relationships between them and us, and their concealed actions on the visible world, and not for the material usefulness we can get from it. From this point of view, no study of any spirit is useless; we can learn something from all of them: their imperfections, flaws, inadequacies and even their ignorance are subjects of observation that initiate us into the study of the inner nature of that world. And when it is not they who educate us through their teachings, it is we who educate ourselves by studying them, just as we do when we study the customs of a people unknown to us.

As for enlightened spirits, they can teach us a great deal, but within the limits of what is possible, and we must not ask them what they cannot or must not reveal to us. We must be content with what they tell us; to want to go any further is to expose ourselves to the hoaxes of frivolous spirits, who are always ready to respond to anything. Experience teaches us how to discern the degree of trust we can put in them.

The Practical Usefulness of Manifestations

Visitor – Supposing that the matter is verified and Spiritism is recognized as a reality, what would its practical usefulness be? If we have done without it until now, it seems to me that we could continue to do without it and still live quite serenely.

A.K. – One could say the same about railroads and steam, without which we used to live very well.

If we understand "practical usefulness" to mean living well, making fortunes, knowing the future, discovering coal mines or hidden treasures, receiving inheritances or saving ourselves from the efforts of doing research, Spiritism serves no one; it can neither raise nor lower the stock market, be transformed into shares, or produce finished inventions ready to be utilized. But how many of our sciences would be useless from that point of view! How many there are with no advantages, commercially speaking! Humans got along perfectly well long before the discovery of all the new planets, before they knew that it is the earth that orbits and not the sun, before eclipses could be calculated, before they knew about the microscopic world, and a hundred other things. In order to live and grow their wheat, peasants don't have to know what a comet is. So why do scholars devote themselves to such research, and who would dare say they are just wasting their time?

Everything that serves to lift a corner of the veil aids the development of our intelligence and enlarges our range of ideas by enabling us to penetrate the laws of nature more deeply. Since the spirit world exists by virtue of one of such laws of nature, Spiritism enables us to know about it. It teaches us the influence that the invisible world exerts on the visible world and the connections between the two in the same way that astronomy teaches us the connections between the stars and the earth. It shows us that invisible world is one of the forces that govern the universe and contributes to maintaining overall harmony. But let's suppose that its usefulness ends there; apart from any moral doctrine, wouldn't the revelation of such a power still be very useful? So, is it really nothing that a whole new world is revealed to us, especially if knowledge about the spirit world puts us on the track of a multitude of up-to-now unsolvable problems? Is it nothing at all that it initiates us into the mysteries beyond the grave, which ought to hold some interest to us because each and everyone must take that fateful step sooner or later? Spiritism has another, more positive usefulness, however: the moral influence it exerts by necessity. Spiritism is the obvious proof of the soul's existence, of its individuality after death, its immortality, and its future destiny; thus, it is the destruction of materialism, not by means of reasoning, but by the facts.

We shouldn't ask Spiritism what it can give, nor look for something in it that is beyond its beneficial purpose. Before the serious progress made in astronomy, people believed in astrology. Would it be reasonable to claim that astronomy is useless because we can no longer find the prediction of our future in the influence of the heavenly bodies? In the same way that astronomy has dethroned the astrologers, Spiritism has dethroned the soothsayers, sorcerers and fortune-tellers. Spiritism is to magic what astronomy is to astrology, and chemistry is to alchemy.

Insanity, Suicide, Obsession

Visitor – Certain people regard Spiritist ideas as likely to disturb the mental faculties, and for that reason they think it prudent to stop its expansion.

A.K. – You know the proverb: When you want to kill a dog, you say it is rabid. So it isn't surprising that the enemies of Spiritism try to lean on any pretext they can. Such a ploy to arouse fear and susceptibilities seemed right to them, and so they eagerly seized upon it; however, their argument collapses under the slightest scrutiny. Consequently, one should look at this "insanity" as the reasoning of the insane.

All great preoccupations of the mind can produce insanity; the sciences, the arts – even religion itself – have provided their fair share. The source of insanity lies in a pathological condition of the brain, the instrument of thought: when the instrument is damaged, thought is impaired. Thus, insanity is a consequential effect, whose primary cause is an organic predisposition that makes the brain susceptible in varying degrees to certain impressions. This is so true that there are people who think a great deal, yet do not go mad, and others that go mad under the influence of the slightest over-excitement. Whenever there is a predisposition toward insanity, it will take on the character of its main concern, which then becomes an *idée fixe*. This *idée fixe* can involve spirits in someone who is preoccupied with spirits, just as it can involve God, angels, the Devil, fortune, power, an art, a science, motherhood, a political or social theory. It is probable that the religious insane would become insane Spiritists if Spiritism happened to be their dominant fixation. Its' true that a newspaper stated that in only one place in America – I cannot recall the name – there were four thousand cases of Spiritist insanity; however, we know that amongst our adversaries it is an *idée fixe* that they consider themselves to be the only ones gifted with reason, and that is a mania like any other. In their eyes, we all deserve to be in an insane asylum, and consequently, those four thousand Spiritists must be crazy as well. If that is the case, the United States has hundreds of thousands of them, and all the other countries in the world an even greater number. This bad tale started to make its rounds after it was noticed that this so-called insanity had reached the highest levels of society. A lot of noise was made about the well-known example of Victor Hennequin[22], but we shouldn't forget that, before concerning himself with Spiritism, he had already demonstrated an unmistakable eccentricity of ideas. If table turning had not happened, which, according to our adversaries' very witty play on words made his head turn, his insanity would have taken another course.

So I will say that Spiritism is in no way privileged in this regard; but I will go even further: I will say that, when well understood, it is actually a protection against insanity and suicide.

Among the most frequent causes of brain over-excitation we must include disappointment, misfortune and thwarted affections,

---

[22] A philosopher, politician, lawyer, and literary man, Victor Hennequin was sent to prison after the French coup of 1851. He had been suffering from schizophrenia, which became worse after he left prison. It was then that he became acquainted with table turning. – Tr.

which are also the most frequent causes of suicide. True Spiritists, however, see the things of this world from such a comprehensive point of view that for them troubles are nothing more than the disagreeable incidents of a journey. That which might cause a violent emotion in others barely affects Spiritists at all. They know, moreover, that life's sufferings are trials that aid their advancement if they bear them without complaining because they will be rewarded according to the courage with which they have endured them. Their convictions thus endow them with a resignation that saves them from despair, and consequently, from an ongoing cause of insanity and suicide. Also, because of what they have seen through communications with spirits, they also know of the deplorable fate of those who intentionally shorten their days, and this picture serves well to make them reflect; hence, the number of those who have opted against choosing that disastrous slope is considerable. This is just one of the results of Spiritism.

To the number of the causes of insanity we must also add fear, and fear of the Devil has deranged more than one mind. Do we perchance know the number of victims created by frightening feeble imaginations with this depiction, made even more frightful with hideous details? The Devil, they say, not only scares children but is also a restraint for them to be good; yes, exactly like the bogey-man and the werewolf, and once they are no longer afraid of them, they become even more ill-behaved than before. And for such a fine result, no one has counted the number of fits caused by the shock to a delicate mind.

We mustn't confuse *pathological insanity* with *obsession*. The latter doesn't originate from any sort of brain injury, but from the control that malevolent spirits exert over certain individuals, and which sometimes has the appearance of insanity per se. This malady, which has nothing to do with any belief in Spiritism, is very common and has always existed. Ordinary medication is powerless and even harmful in such a case. Spiritism has made this new cause of the disorder known while at the same time offering the only way to overcome it by acting not on the patient, but on the obsessor spirit. It is the remedy for, and not the cause of the ailment.

Forgetfulness of the Past

Visitor – I don't understand how people can benefit from the experience acquired in their past lives if they cannot remember them. Each new existence is as if it were the very first, and therefore they are always having to start all over again. Let's suppose that every day when we wake up we forget what we did the day before; we would have made no more progress by the time we reach seventy years of age than we did at ten. But since we do remember our wrongs, our imperfections and the punishments we have incurred, we make sure that we do not have to start all over again. To use your comparison of equating a person on earth with a high school student, I cannot understand what this student could gain from his fourth grade studies, for example, if he can't remember what he learned in third grade. These breaks in the continuity of the spirit's life interrupt all its relationships, and in a matter of speaking, make it a new being. What we may conclude is that our memories die with each existence; hence, we are born without any awareness of what we have been. It is a kind of nothingness.

A.K. – From question to question, you are leading me to give you a complete course on Spiritism since all the objections you have raised are natural for someone who knows nothing about it. An earnest study of Spiritism, however, could provide a much fuller view than I can in a brief explanation, which, in and of itself, will raise even more issues. Everything is connected in Spiritism, and when we follow the whole, we see that the principles follow one from the other, and mutually support one another. Then, what appears to be an anomaly that is contrary to God's justice and wisdom seems completely natural and confirms such justice and wisdom.

Such is the problem of the forgetfulness of the past, which is connected to other questions of equal importance, and that is why I will touch on it only briefly here.

If with every existence a veil is thrown over the past, the spirit loses nothing of what it acquired in that past: it forgets only the way in which it acquired it. To use the comparison of the student, I would say that it makes little difference to him to know where, how, and under what teacher he completed the third grade if upon reaching the fourth he knows what he learned in the third. Why should it matter to him to know if he had been punished for his laziness and disobedience if such punishments made him hard-working and well-behaved? Thus it is that upon reincarnating, persons bring through intuition and innate ideas what they have acquired in knowledge and morality. I say "in morality" because if they improved themselves during a lifetime and if they benefited from the lessons of experience, then upon returning, they will be instinctively better; matured in the school of suffering, and through work, their spirits will be stronger. Rather than having to start everything all over again, they will possess an increasingly richer basis upon which to rely in order to acquire even more.

The second part of your objection – the wiping out of memories – is no better founded, because this forgetfulness takes place only during corporeal life. Upon leaving it, the spirit recovers the memory of its past and can then judge the path it has taken and what still remains for it to do; hence, there is no breach of continuity in the spirit life, which is the normal life of the spirit.

Temporary forgetfulness is a gift from Providence. Experience is often acquired through harsh trials and terrible expiations, and remembering them would be very painful and would add to the troubles of our present life. If the sufferings of life seem long, what would it be like if their duration were increased with the memory of sufferings from past lives? For example, today you are an honest man, but perhaps you owe it to the harsh punishments you experienced for a wrong you committed in the past that would be repugnant to your conscience now. Would it be pleasant for you to remember having been hanged for it? Wouldn't shame haunt you, thinking that everyone knows about the wrong you committed? What does it matter to you what you were capable of doing and what you may have endured in expiation if you are now a person worthy of esteem? In the eyes of the world, you are a new person, and in the eyes of God, a rehabilitated spirit. Free from the memory of a troublesome past, you act with more freedom; it is a new beginning for you; your old debts are paid and it is up to you not to incur new ones.

During their present lives, how many persons would love to be able to throw a veil over their early years! How many have said at the end of their lives, "If I had it to do all over again, I certainly wouldn't do what I did!" Well then! What they cannot redo in this lifetime, they will redo in another; in a new existence, their spirit will bring with it through intuition the good decisions they made in the past. This is how human progress is gradually accomplished.

Let us suppose further – and this is very common – that in your relationships, maybe in your own family, there is someone you had much to complain about in a past life; someone who perhaps ruined or dishonored you, and now, as a repentant spirit, has come to incarnate in your midst, to unite with you through family ties to make amends by way of his or her current devotion and affection for the evil done to you in the past. Wouldn't it be very awkward for both of you if you both remembered your enmity? Instead of being abated, the hatred would be perpetuated.

We may conclude from this that the remembrance of the past would greatly upset social relations and would be an obstacle to progress. Do you want actual proof? A man condemned to prison makes a firm resolution to become honest; what will become of him once released? He will be rejected by society, and this rejection will plunge him again into vice. Suppose, on the other hand, that no one is aware of his past; he will be well-received. If he himself is able to forget his past, he will be no less honest and will be able to walk with his head held high instead of bent under the shame of his memories.

This agrees perfectly with the Spirits' doctrine about worlds that are more highly evolved than ours. On such worlds, where only the good reigns, remembrance of the past is not at all painful; that is why spirits on them can remember their previous lives as easily as we remember what we did yesterday. As for the sojourns they may have made on lower worlds, they are nothing more than a bad dream.

Elements of Conviction

Visitor – I would agree, sir, that from a philosophical point of view, the Spiritist doctrine is perfectly rational. But there is still the matter of the manifestations, which cannot be resolved except by the phenomena themselves; it is precisely the reality of these phenomena that many people dispute and you should not find it surprising that they would like to witness them.

A.K. – I do think that is quite natural; however, since I want to make the most of this opportunity, I will explain what conditions are best for observing the phenomena, and especially for understanding them. Those who do not want to observe them under such conditions do not have a true desire to learn, so it would be useless to waste our time on them.

You will also agree, sir, that it would be strange indeed if a rational philosophy had emerged from illusory and fabricated occurrences. In good logic, the reality of the effect implies the reality of the cause; if one is true, the other cannot be false, because where there is no tree, no fruit can be gathered.

It is true that not everyone has been able to confirm the phenomena because not everyone has met the conditions needed to observe them or has had the necessary patience and perseverance. The same applies here as in all the sciences: what some do not do, others will. Every day, we accept astronomical calculations without having made them ourselves. Be that as it may, if you find a particular philosophy to be good, you will accept it as you would any other, but you will reserve your opinion about the ways and means that have led to it, or at least accept it as a hypothesis until fully verified.

The elements of conviction are not the same for everyone; what convinces some makes no impression on others – and that is why we must have a little of everything. But it is wrong to believe that physical experiences are the only means of convincing someone. I have seen persons unmoved by the most remarkable phenomena but convinced by a simple written response. When we see a phenomenon that we do not understand, the more extraordinary it is the more suspicious it seems, and our minds always look for an ordinary cause behind it. If we do understand it, however, we accept it more easily because it has a reason for being and the extraordinary and supernatural vanish. Indeed, the explanations I have just given you in this interview are far from being complete; but as abridged as they may be, I am persuaded that they will give you something to think about; and if circumstances enable you to witness any incidents of manifestation, you will see them with a less biased eye because you will have a basis for your reasoning.

There are two aspects to Spiritism: the experimental part, involving the manifestations, and the philosophical doctrine. I am visited by people every day who have not seen anything but who believe as firmly as I do simply because of the study they have made of the philosophical part; for them, the phenomena involving the manifestations is secondary. The foundation is the doctrine, the science. They see it as so great, so rational, that they find in it everything conducive to satisfying their inner yearnings, apart from the manifestations. They have concluded that even if there were no manifestations at all the Spiritist Doctrine would nonetheless be the one that best resolves a multitude of problems thought unsolvable. How many have stated that similar ideas had been brewing in their minds but had remained unclear. Spiritism stated such ideas precisely and gave them a form, and it was like a flash of light. This explains the number of adherents won over by a single reading of *The Spirits' Book*. Do you think that would have been the case if Spiritism hadn't gone beyond the turning and talking tables?

Visitor – You were right in saying that the turning tables gave rise to a philosophical doctrine, and I am far from suspecting the consequences that could arise from something regarded as a simple object of curiosity. I can now see how vast the field opened up by your system is.

A.K. – I would stop you there, sir; you accord me way too much honor by attributing this system to me, because it is not mine. It has been deduced in full from the Spirits' teachings. I only saw, observed and coordinated, and I am now trying to help others understand what I myself do; that is the full lot that has fallen to me. There is this crucial difference between Spiritism and other philosophical systems: the latter are the work of persons who were enlightened to varying degrees, whereas personally, I haven't been worthy of inventing one single principle regarding what you attribute to me. They say: the philosophy of Plato, Descartes and Leibnitz; they will not say: the doctrine of Allan Kardec. That is fortunate because what importance could a name have in such a serious matter? Spiritism has vastly superior auxiliaries, next to whom we are but atoms.

Society for the Continuation of the Spiritist Works of Allan Kardec, 7 de Lille Street

Visitor – You have a society that concerns itself with these studies; would it be possible for me to be a member?

A.K. – Certainly not, at least for the time being. Even though applicants don't have to have a doctorate in Spiritism in order to be accepted, their ideas must at least be more settled on the subject than yours are. Since the Society doesn't want to be disturbed during its study times, it cannot admit those who would come to waste its time on elementary questions, nor those who, unsympathetic toward its principles and beliefs, would incite disorder through untimely arguments or a spirit of conflict. Like so many others, it is a scientific society that concerns itself with delving into the different points of the Spiritist science, and which seeks to become enlightened. It is the center where information is received from all over the world, and where topics related to the progress of the science are delineated and coordinated. But it is not a school, nor is it a course of elementary instruction. Later, when your convictions have been formed by study, we will see if there is room to admit you. Nevertheless, while waiting, you will be able to attend once or twice at the most as a visitor, on the condition that you harbor no thought that could offend anyone; otherwise, because I was the one who will have introduced you, I would incur the reproach of my colleagues and the door would be forever closed to you. You will find it to be a gathering of serious and distinguished men and women, most of whom have been recommended due to the superiority of their knowledge and their social stance, and who would not allow those admitted to deviate from propriety in the least. You mustn't think that the public is invited and that just anyone will be permitted to attend the sessions. Since the Society doesn't put on demonstrations with the idea of satisfying people's curiosity, it is careful to turn away the curious. So, those who think they might find a diversion or some kind of spectacle would be disappointed and would do better not to come at all. That is why the Society refuses to admit, even as simple observers, those it does not know or whose hostile dispositions are well-known.

The Prohibition against Spiritism

Visitor – One last question, if you please. Spiritism has powerful enemies; couldn't they prohibit its practice and its societies, and thereby stop its spread?

A.K. – They would only defeat themselves a little faster because the use of force is the argument of those who have nothing good to say. If Spiritism is a passing fancy, it will fall by itself without anyone having to go to so much trouble; if they persecute it, it is because they fear it, and they fear only what is authentic. If it is a reality, it is, as I have already said, a part of nature itself, and a law of nature cannot be revoked with the stroke of a pen.

If Spirit manifestations were the privilege of one individual, there's no doubt that if that individual were gotten out of the way, it would put an end to the manifestations. Unfortunately for its opponents, such manifestations are not a mystery to anyone; there is nothing secret or occult; everything happens in the full light of day; they are at everyone's disposal, from the palace to the hovel. One might prohibit obtaining them in public, but we know for certain that it is not in public that they are best produced, but in private. Therefore, since anyone may be a medium, who could prevent a family in their home, an individual in the silence of his or her own study, or the prisoner who is locked away, from communicating with spirits without the henchmen's knowledge and right under their noses? Even if a government were strong enough to put a stop to them, would it be able to stop its neighbors and the entire world since there is not a single country in the two hemispheres where there are no mediums?

Furthermore, Spiritism's source is not to be found among humans; it is the work of the Spirits, who can neither be burned nor put in prison. It rests on individual belief and not on societies, which are not necessary. If they succeeded in destroying all the Spiritist books, the Spirits would dictate them all over again.

To sum up, Spiritism today is an assured fact; it has won its place in the public eye and among philosophical doctrines. Therefore, those who do not appreciate it must be prepared to see it all around them, even though they are perfectly free not to accept it.

Third Dialogue

The Priest

A Priest – Would you kindly permit me to ask you a few questions on my part?

Allan Kardec. – Gladly. But before answering you, I think I should let you know how I intend to discuss matters with you.

First, I must say that I have no intention whatsoever of converting you to our ideas. If you want to know about them in detail, you will find them in the books where they have already been explained. You can study them at your leisure and feel free to accept or reject them.

The goal of Spiritism is to combat disbelief and its disastrous consequences while providing obvious proofs for the existence of the soul and future life. It thus speaks to those who believe in nothing at all *or those who doubt;* and their numbers are large, as you know. Those who have religious faith, and for whom *such faith is sufficient*, do not need Spiritism. To those who say, "I believe in the authority of the Church and I shall hold to what it teaches, without looking further," Spiritism replies that it does not impose itself on anyone and has not come to force any conviction.

Freedom of conscience is one consequence of freedom of thought, which is one of the attributes of human beings; Spiritism would be in conflict with its own principles of charity and tolerance if it did not respect this freedom. For Spiritism, every belief, if it is sincere and does not lead people to do wrong to their neighbor, is respectable, even if erroneous. For example, if people were to find their consciences telling them to believe that it is the sun that orbits around the earth, we would say to them: Believe it if you like, because it will not keep the earth from orbiting the sun. Just as we do not try to violate your conscience, do not try to violate other people's consciences. If you make an innocuous belief into an instrument of persecution, it becomes harmful and should be opposed.

That, Reverend, is the line of conduct I have followed with the clergy of several denominations who have addressed me. When they question me about certain points of the Doctrine, I provide them with the explanations they need, but I avoid arguing about certain dogmas that Spiritism is not concerned with; thus, they are all free to make their own evaluations. However, I have never sought them out with the desire to undermine their faith through any kind of pressure. Those who come to us as brothers, we welcome as brothers; those who reject us, we leave in peace. This is the advice I always give to Spiritists because I have never approved of those who believe it their mission to convert the clergy. I always tell them: Sow in the field of the disbelievers because there is an ample harvest to gather.

Spiritism does not impose itself because, as I have said, it respects freedom of conscience. Moreover, it understands that any imposed belief is superficial and gives only the appearances of faith, but it is not real faith. It lays out its principles in front of everyone so that all may form an opinion with full knowledge of the facts. Those who accept its principles, whether they are clergy or laity, do so freely because they find them to be rational. But we in no way trouble ourselves with those who are not of our opinion. If there is a struggle between the Church and Spiritism nowadays, we know that we are not the ones who caused it.

Priest – If the Church sees the rise of a new doctrine and believes its principles condemnable according to the Church's conscience, do you question its right to discuss them and fight them, and to caution the faithful against what it regards as error?

A.K. – In no way do we question a right that we ourselves claim. If the Church would confine itself to the limits of the discussion, there would be nothing to be concerned about. But read most of the writings issued by its members or published in the name of religion, in addition to the sermons that have been preached, and you will see offense and slander bursting forth far and wide, and the principles of the Doctrine undeservedly and maliciously misrepresented. Haven't we heard from atop the pulpit that its adherents are enemies of society and the public order? That those whom it has brought back to the faith are to be anathematized and rejected by the Church because it is better to be a disbeliever than to believe in God and the soul through Spiritism? Hasn't it been lamented that there are no Inquisition-type burnings-at-the-stake for Spiritists? In certain locations, haven't they singled them out for the reprehension of their fellow citizens, even urging them to pursue and insult them in the streets? Haven't they enjoined all the faithful to flee from them like the plague, dissuading domestic servants from going to work for them? Haven't women been urged to leave their husbands, and husbands to leave their wives because of Spiritism? Haven't they caused employees to lose their jobs, depriving workers of their wages and the unfortunate of the bread of charity because they are Spiritists? Haven't they even sent the blind away from certain almshouses because they wouldn't renounce their beliefs? Tell me, Reverend, is that fair treatment? Have Spiritists answered insult with insult, wrong with wrong? No. They have applied calm and moderation. Public awareness has already absolved them of being the aggressors.

Priest – Any sane person would deplore such excesses, but the Church shouldn't be held responsible for the abuses committed by some of its less informed members.

A. K. – I agree, but aren't these less informed members the leaders of the Church? Look at the pastoral letter of the Bishop of Algiers[23] and a few others. Wasn't it a bishop who ordered the book-burning in Barcelona?[24] Don't the higher level ecclesiastical authorities have all the power over their subordinates? If the Church thus tolerates sermons unworthy of the evangelical pulpit, if it favors the publication of offensive and defamatory writings against a class of citizens, and if it does not oppose persecutions practiced in the name of religion, it is because it approves of them.

In sum, by systematically turning away Spiritists who return to it, the Church has forced them to withdraw unto themselves. By the nature and violence of its attacks, it has widened the discussion and taken it to new ground. Spiritism is merely a philosophical doctrine; it is the Church itself that has caused it to grow by presenting it as a dreaded enemy. Lastly, it is the Church itself that has proclaimed it a new religion. That was a blunder, but passion does not reason.

A Free Thinker – You have proclaimed freedom of thought and conscience and have declared that every sincere belief is respectable. Materialism is a belief like any other; why shouldn't it enjoy the freedom you grant to all the others?

A.K. – Everyone is certainly free to believe as they please or to believe in nothing at all, and we would no more excuse persecution against those who believe in nothingness after death than against a schismatic from any religion. In combating materialism, we attack

---

[23] "Circular Letter and Ordinance of the Bishop of Algiers on the Superstition called Spiritualism" – August 18, 1863, signed by Louis Antoine-Augustin, Bishop of Algiers. – Tr.

[24] A modern-day book-burning held on the morning of October 9, 1861 on the Barcelona Esplanade. The difference between this burning and the fiery executions of earlier centuries was that the early victims were humans, while these were all the books, pamphlets, and works of a Spiritualist character that could be found at that period of the movement. Resting on the "funeral pyre" were the writings of Allan Kardec and Baron Ludwig von Guldenstubbe, some copies of English and American Spiritualist papers, and a large collection of tracts issued by Spaning Spiritualists. http://www.novelguide.com/a/ discover/eop_02/eop_02_04226.html. – Tr.

not individuals, but a doctrine, which, if harmless to society when confined to the conscience of educated people, turns into a social calamity if it becomes widespread.

The belief that everything ends for human beings at death, that all solidarity ceases when physical life ceases, leads us to regard sacrificing our present welfare on behalf of someone else as pure nonsense; hence the maxim: "Every man for himself because there is nothing after this life." In other words, charity, fraternity and morality have no basis, no reason for being. Why inconvenience, restrain and deprive ourselves today, when tomorrow, perhaps, we will be no more? The denial of the future and the mere doubt about the future life are the greatest stimulants of selfishness, the source of most of humankind's ills. A great deal of virtue is needed to keep us from falling into vice and crime, with no restraint other than our will-power. Human respect might restrain men and women of the world, but not those for whom the fear of public opinion is nil.

Belief in the future life, demonstrating the continuation of relationships between individuals, establishes a solidarity that does not stop at the grave; thus, it changes the course of ideas. If this belief were nothing but a "man of straw," it would be temporary; but since its reality is a fact derived from experience, then, in the interest of the social order, it is an obligation to spread it and strive against the opposite belief. This is what Spiritism does, and it does so with success because it provides proof, and because people would surely prefer the certainty of the continuation of life and of being able to live happily on a better world as compensation for the miseries of this one, as opposed to believing in being dead forever. The thought of being erased from existence forever, of believing that their children and those dear to them are lost with no possibility of coming back, puts a smile on a very small number of faces, believe me. That is why attacks against Spiritism in the name of disbelief have had such little success and have not weakened it for an instant.

Priest – Religion teaches all of that, and until now it has been sufficient. Why is there a need for a new doctrine?

A.K. – If religion is sufficient, why are there so many disbelievers, religiously speaking? It is true that religion teaches us and tells us to believe, but there are so many people who do not believe in words alone! Spiritism proves and enables us to see what religion teaches through theory. Moreover, where do these proofs come from? From spirit manifestations. Well now, it is likely that spirits manifest only with God's permission; thus, if God, out of divine mercy, sends this aid to people to draw them out of disbelief, it would be impious to reject it.

Priest – But you cannot deny the fact that Spiritism is not in agreement with religion on all points.

A.K – Goodness, Reverend! All religions say the same thing: Protestantism, Judaism, Islam, as well as Catholicism.

If Spiritism denied the existence of God, the soul, the soul's individuality and immortality, future rewards and punishments, and free will; if it taught that we are on this world only for ourselves and that we should think only of ourselves, it would not be only contrary to Catholicism, but all the religions of the world; it would be the negation of all moral laws, the foundations of human society. Far from it. The Spirits proclaim a sole God who is supremely just and good. They say that human beings are free and are responsible for their actions, and that they are rewarded and punished according to the good or evil they have done. They place above all other virtues evangelical charity and this sublime rule taught by Christ: "Do unto others as you would have them do unto you." Aren't these the foundations of every religion? And the Spirits have done even more: they have initiated us into the mysteries of the future life, which for us is no longer an abstraction but a reality. Those whom we ourselves once knew have come back to describe their situations to us and to tell us how and why they suffer or are happy. What is anti-religious about that? This certainty of the future, of meeting our loved ones once again – is that not comforting? Isn't the magnificence of the spirit life – which is our essence – compared with the paltry anxieties of earthly life enough to make us lift up our souls and to encourage us toward the good?

Priest – Regarding general matters, I agree that Spiritism is consistent with the great truths of Christianity; but does the same apply from the dogma point of view? Doesn't it contradict certain principles that the Church teaches us?

A.K. – Spiritism is, above all, a science and does not concern itself with dogmatic issues at all. This science has moral consequences as do all philosophical sciences. Are these consequences good or bad? We can judge them by the general principles I just mentioned. A lot of people are mistaken about the true character of Spiritism. The matter is serious enough to merit some further discussion.

First, let us cite a comparison: electricity, present in nature, has existed throughout time, and throughout time it has produced the effects that we are familiar with and many that we are not yet familiar with. Ignorant of the true cause, people used to explain these effects in a more or less bizarre way. The discovery of electricity and its properties has undermined a host of absurd theories, while shedding light on more than one of nature's mysteries. What electricity and the physical sciences in general have done for certain phenomena, Spiritism has done for phenomena of a different order.

Spiritism is founded on the existence of an invisible world made up of incorporeal beings who populate space, and who are none other than the souls of those who used to live on the earth or on other spheres, where they left their material envelopes behind.

We call these beings *spirits*. They surround us continuously, exerting a great influence on people without them even being aware of it; they play a very active role in the mental world, and up to a point in the physical world. Spiritism is therefore contained in nature, and we may say that, for a certain order of ideas, it is a power, just as electricity is a power from another point of view, and gravity from yet another. The phenomena, whose source is the invisible world, have in fact been produced throughout time; that is why the history of every culture mentions them. As with electricity, only in their ignorance did people attribute these phenomena to more or less-rational causes and give free reign to their imaginations regarding them.

Spiritism has been studied more thoroughly since its popularization and has shed light on a multitude of questions formerly insolvable or misunderstood. Its true character is therefore that of a science and not of a religion, and the proof is that it counts among its adherents people of all faiths who have not had to renounce their convictions because of it: devout Catholics who do not in any way neglect all the duties of their creed – as long as they are not rebuffed by their Church; Protestants of all denominations, Jews, Muslims, even Buddhists and Brahmans.

Therefore, Spiritism rests on principles independent of any dogmatic nature. Its moral consequences are those found in Christianity because Christianity is the clearest and purest of all doctrines. Furthermore, it is for this reason that, of all the religious sects in the world, Christians are the most capable of understanding Spiritism in its true essence. Can we blame it because of this? Of course, everyone can make a religion of their opinions and interpret known religions as they please, but from there to establishing a new church there is a great distance.

Priest – But don't you perform evocations according to some religious formula?

A.K. – Of course, we bring a religious sentiment to the evocations and to our meetings, but there is no sacramental formula; for spirits, thought is everything and form is nothing. We call them in God's name because we believe in God and we know that nothing is done in this world without his permission, and that if God does not allow them to come, they will not come. We proceed with our work calmly and thoughtfully, first because it is a necessary condition for observations, and second because we know the respect we owe to those who no longer live on earth, whatever their circumstances may be, happy or unhappy, in the spirit world. We evoke good spirits because, knowing there are good ones and evil ones, we do not want the latter to come and interfere deceitfully in the communications we receive. What does all this prove? That we are not atheists, but it does not at all imply that we are religionists.

Priest – Well then! What do the high order spirits say about religion? The good ones ought to advise and guide us. Suppose I have no religion and I want to choose one. What would they say if I were to ask them: Would you advise me to become a Catholic, Protestant, Anglican, Quaker, Jew, Muslim or Mormon?

A.K. – There are two points to consider regarding religions: the general principles common to all of them, and the principles peculiar to each one. The former are those we have been speaking of thus far; those that all spirits proclaim, regardless of their order. As for the latter, *average* spirits, although not evil, may have preferences and opinions; they may advocate this or that form. Thus, they may encourage certain practices either from personal conviction, whether from ideas retained from earthly life, or whether out of prudence so as not to frighten timid consciences. Do you believe, for example, that an enlightened spirit – maybe Fenelon himself – in addressing Muslims would tell them inappropriately that Mohammed was an impostor, and that they will be damned if they do not become Christians? He would refrain from doing so, because he would be rejected.

In general, when not asked to address a matter specifically, high order spirits do not concern themselves with particulars. They limit themselves to saying: "God is good and just; God wants only the good." The best of all religions, therefore, is that which teaches only what conforms to God's goodness and justice; which entails the broadest, most sublime idea about God and does not lessen him by attributing human narrow-mindedness and passions to him; which renders people good and virtuous and teaches them all to love each other as brothers and sisters; which condemns every wrong done to one's neighbor; which does not authorize injustice under any form or pretext; which does not prescribe anything contrary to the immutable laws of nature, for God cannot contradict himself; whose clergy embody the best example of goodness, charity, and morality; the one that best pursues the struggle against selfishness and least flatters people's pride and vanity; and lastly, in whose name the least amount of evil is committed, for a good religion cannot be the pretext for any evil whatsoever – it must not leave any door open to it, either directly or by interpretation. Observe, judge and choose.

Priest – I suppose that certain points of the Catholic doctrine are contested by spirits you regard as being of a high order. I suppose that these points may actually be erroneous; according to these same spirits, for those for whom they are articles of faith – whether right or wrong – and who practice them accordingly, can such a belief be harmful to their salvation?

A.K. – Certainly not, if such belief does not deter them from doing good, and if, on the contrary, it prompts them to do so. On the other hand, the best-founded belief will obviously harm their faith if it gives them occasion to do evil, to be lacking in charity toward their neighbor, and if it makes them hard and selfish, because then they are not acting according to the law of God, and God considers thoughts before acts. Who would dare think otherwise?

For example, regarding those who might believe wholeheartedly in God, but in God's name commit acts that are inhumane or contrary to charity, do you think that their faith will do them any good? Aren't they all the more blameworthy because their means of being enlightened are all the greater?

Priest – So devoted Catholics who scrupulously fulfill the duties of their creed are not condemned by the Spirits?

A.K. – No, if it is a matter of conscience for them, and if they do so with sincerity. But yes – a thousand times yes – if it is out of hypocrisy, and if it displays only the appearance of piety.

High order spirits, those whose mission is the progress of humankind, rise up against every abuse that might hinder such progress, regardless of the nature of the abuse and regardless of which individuals or social classes may profit from it. Now you cannot deny the fact that religion has not always been exempt from this. Even if among its clergy there are those who fulfill their mission with true Christian devotion, who render their mission grand, beautiful and respectable, you will have to agree that not all have always fulfilled the sanctity of their ministry. The Spirits are opposed to evil wherever it may be found. Is pointing out the abuses of religion the same as attacking it? Religion has no greater enemies than those who defend such abuses, for they are what give rise to the thought that something better can replace it. If religion is in danger, we have to lay the blame on those who offer a false idea of it, transforming it into a battleground of human passions, and who exploit it to further their ambitions.

Priest – You say that Spiritism does not argue over dogma, and yet it accepts certain points contested by the Church, such as reincarnation and the presence of humans on the earth before Adam. It also denies eternal punishment, the existence of demons, purgatory, and the fires of hell.

A.K. – These points have been argued over for a long time, and it is not only Spiritism that has questioned them; they are merely opinions, some of which are considered controversial even by theology and which only the future will settle. One great principle governs them all: the practice of the good, which is the higher law, the essential *sine qua non* condition for our future, as proved by the condition of the spirits who communicate with us. While waiting for light to be shed on these questions, believe, if you wish, in flames and material tortures if doing so keeps you from doing evil. But that will not render them more real if they do not actually exist. Believe that we have only one corporeal existence if it pleases you: that will not prevent you from being born again here or elsewhere if that is really the way it is, and despite what you might think. Believe that the world was fully created in six twenty-four hour days if that is your opinion: that will not keep the earth from bearing proof to the contrary in its geological layers. Believe, if you wish, that Joshua stopped the sun: that will not stop the earth in its orbit. Believe that humankind has been on the earth for only 6,000 years: that will not keep the facts from showing that that is impossible. And what would you say if one fine day this inexorable geology produces obvious evidence that demonstrates the anteriority of humankind, just as it has demonstrated so many other things? So believe in anything you like, even in the Devil, if such belief enables you to be good, humane and charitable toward your fellow beings. As a moral doctrine, Spiritism imposes only one thing: the necessity of doing good and not doing evil. It is a science of observation, which, I repeat, has moral consequences, and these consequences are the confirmation and proof of the great principles of religion. As for the secondary questions, it leaves those to each one's conscience.

Be mindful of the fact, sir, that Spiritism does not dispute in principle some of the different points of which you just spoke. If you had read everything that I have written on the subject, you would have seen that it is limited to giving such points a more logical and rational explanation than the one commonly given. This is why it does not deny purgatory, for example; on the contrary, it demonstrates its necessity and justice. But it does even more – it defines what purgatory is. Hell has been described as an immense furnace, but is that really how scholarly theology understands it? Obviously not; it says quite clearly that it is merely a symbol and that the fire in which one burns is a mental fire, a symbol of the greatest sorrows.

As for eternal punishment, if it were possible to survey the personal opinion of all individuals in a position to reason or understand – even among the most devout – we would see on what side the majority is because the idea of eternal torment is a denial of God's infinite mercy.

Moreover, let's see what the Spiritist doctrine says on the subject:

The length of the punishment depends on the improvement of the guilty spirit. No condemnation for a set time is pronounced against it. What God requires of it to bring its suffering to an end is repentance, expiation, and *reparation;* in other words, a serious, effective improvement and a sincere return to the good. The spirit is thus the arbiter of its own fate; it can prolong its suffering by its obstinacy in evil, or it can mitigate or shorten it through its efforts to do good.

Since the length of the punishment depends on repentance, it follows that the guilty spirit who did not repent and never improved itself would continue to suffer, and that for it, the punishment would be eternal. Eternal punishment should thus be understood in the relative and not the absolute sense.

A condition inherent to low order spirits is that they cannot see the end of their situation and so they think that they will have to suffer forever; for them it is a punishment. But as soon as their soul opens up to repentance, God enables them to glimpse a ray of hope.

This doctrine obviously conforms more to God's justice, which punishes as long as we persist in evil and pardons when we enter the path of the good. Who devised this doctrine? Was it us? No. It was the Spirits, who teach and demonstrate it by the examples they set before us each and every day.

Therefore, spirits do not deny future punishment – they have described their own sufferings; and this description has more impact on us than that of never-ending fire, because everything about it is perfectly logical. We understand that it is possible, that it must be so, and that such a situation is a completely natural consequence of things; it can be accepted by the philosophical thinker because there is nothing about it that clashes with reason. That is why Spiritist beliefs have brought a multitude of people back to the good – even materialists, whom the fear of hell, as it has been depicted, had not been able to restrain.

Priest – Even if I were to accept your reasoning, don't you think ordinary people need images that are more frightening than a philosophy they can't understand?

A.K. – That is an error that has created more than one materialist, or at the very least, has turned more than one person away from religion. There comes a time when such images are no longer frightening, and then people who do not bother to delve into the matter more deeply after rejecting one aspect end up rejecting the whole and say to themselves: If they have taught me a false principle as an indisputable truth, if they have given me an image, a symbol as being the reality, who says the rest is any more truthful? On the contrary, if reason, as it increases, does not reject anything, faith is strengthened thereby. Religion will always gain by following the progress of ideas. If someday it runs into peril, it will be because humans have advanced while it has remained behind. It is a mistake in this day and age to believe that people can be led by means of fear of the Devil and eternal tortures.

Priest – The Church indeed recognizes nowadays that physical hell is just a symbol, but that does not rule out the existence of demons; without them, how can one explain the influence of evil, which cannot come from God?

A.K. – Spiritism does not believe in demons in the popular sense of the word, but it does believe in evil spirits who are no better and who do as much harm by arousing evil thoughts. Spiritism only states that these are not separate beings, created for evil and perpetually devoted to it as some kind of outcasts of creation and tormentors of humankind. They are less-evolved, still-imperfect beings, but for whom God reserves a future. That is in agreement with the Orthodox Church, which believes in the conversion of Satan, an allusion to the improvement of evil spirits. Note further that the word *demon* does not imply the idea of evil spirits except through the modern meaning that has been given to it, because the Greek word *daimon* means *genius, intelligence*. Now, to admit communications from evil spirits is to recognize in principle the reality of spirit manifestations. Next, we must find out if only evil spirits communicate, which the Church uses as its reason to prohibit communicating with spirits. Here we call upon both reasoning and the facts. If spirits, whatever they may be, communicate, it is only with God's permission: are we to understand that God allows only the evil ones to communicate? How could that be? If he gives them full liberty to come and deceive humans, would he prohibit the good ones from coming as a counterweight to neutralize their pernicious teachings? Wouldn't believing such a thing call into question God's power and goodness and make Satan a rival to the Divinity? The Bible, the Gospel and the Church Fathers fully recognize the possibility of communicating with the invisible world, and that good spirits are not excluded from that world; so why would they be excluded nowadays? Moreover, by accepting the authenticity of certain apparitions and communications from the saints, the Church is thus rejecting the idea that we can communicate only with evil spirits. When communications contain only good things; when they preach the purest and most sublime evangelical morals, selflessness, disinterest and love toward our neighbor; when they fight evil, no matter in what shade it presents itself, is it really rational to believe that malicious spirits have thereby come to perform their work?

Priest – The New Testament teaches us that the angel of darkness, or Satan, can transform himself into an angel of light to seduce people.

A.K. – According to Spiritism and the opinion of many Christian philosophers, Satan is not a real being; he is the personification of evil, just as Saturn used to be the personification of time. The Church takes this allegorical figure literally; it is a matter of opinion that I will not discuss. Let us say, for a moment, that Satan is a real being; by exaggerating his power in order to frighten people, the Church achieves a completely different result, i.e. one of the destruction not only of all fear, but also of all belief in his person, according to the proverb: "Those who wish to prove too much prove nothing at all." The Church represents Satan as eminently clever, skilful, and cunning; however, when it comes to Spiritism, the Church makes him play the role of an inept and a fool.

Since Satan's goal is to feed hell with his victims and to steal souls from God, we can see why he busies himself with those who are on the path of the good to lead them into evil. And to do so, according to a beautiful allegory, he transforms himself into an angel of light; that is, he hypocritically feigns virtue; what is incomprehensible, however, is why he would let those he already has in his clutches escape. Those who believe in neither God nor the soul, who scorn prayer and are immersed in vice, already belong to Satan as much as is possible. He has nothing further to do to sink them deeper in the mire; thus, to encourage them to return to God, to pray to him, to submit to his will, and to encourage them to renounce evil while showing them the happiness of the elect and the sad fate that awaits the wicked would be the act of a fool, which would be more stupid than if we were to give freedom to caged birds with the thought of catching them again afterward.

Therefore, in the doctrine of exclusive communication with demons, there is a contradiction that strikes all sensible people. That is why no one could ever be persuaded that spirits who lead back to God those who used to deny him and used to do evil; that spirits who console the afflicted, give strength and courage to the weak, and who, by the sublimity of their teachings, raise the soul above material life, are Satan's accomplices, and that on such grounds we ought to interdict all relations with the invisible world.

Priest – If the Church forbids communications with the spirits of the dead, it is because they are against religion, since they are formally condemned by the Gospels and by Moses. The latter, declaring the death penalty against such practices, proves how reprehensible they are in God's eyes.

A.K. – I beg your pardon, but this prohibition is not found anywhere in the Gospels; it is found only in the Mosaic Law. It is thus a matter of knowing if the Church puts the Mosaic Law above the law of the Gospels; or to put it another way, if the Church is more Jewish than Christian. It is also worth noting that of all religions, the one that opposes Spiritism the least is Judaism, and that it has not resorted to the Mosaic Law, upon which Christian denominations rest their opinion, to prohibit evocations. If biblical instructions are the code of the Christian faith, why prohibit the reading of the Bible? What would be said of forbidding a citizen from studying the law code of his or her own country?

The reason for Moses' prohibition was that the Hebrew lawmaker wanted his people to break with all the customs they had acquired while among the Egyptians, and the one we are discussing here was a subject of abuse. The dead were not evoked out of respect and affection for them, or out of a sentiment of piety, but as a means of fortunetelling, the object of shameful dealings exploited by charlatanism and superstition. Moses was therefore right to prohibit it. If he pronounced a severe punishment against this abuse, it was because he needed harsh means to govern his unruly people; also, the death penalty was widely used in his lawmaking. One wrongly leans on the severity of the punishment in order to prove the degree of culpability in evoking the dead.

If the argument against evoking the dead comes from God himself – as the Church claims – it must have been God who decreed the penalty of death against offenders. The death penalty therefore has an origin as sacred as the prohibition. So why hasn't it been preserved? Moses promulgated all his laws in the name of God and under God's orders. If we believe that God is their author, why are they no longer observed? If Moses' law is for the Church an article of faith at one point, why isn't it an article of faith at every point? Why resort to it for what we need, but then reject it when it is unsuitable? Why not follow all its regulations; for instance, circumcision, to which Jesus himself submitted and did not abolish?

There were two parts to the Mosaic Law: first, the law of God, summarized in the Sinai tablets, which has remained because it is divine, and which Christ only developed further; second, the civil or criminal law, appropriate for the customs of the time, and which Christ abolished.

Today, circumstances are no longer the same, and Moses' prohibition has no reason to be. Moreover, if the Church forbids evoking spirits, can it prevent them from coming without being called? Every day, don't we see people who have never been involved in Spiritism, and who knew nothing about it before it was divulged, experiencing manifestations of all kinds?

Another contradiction: if Moses prohibited evoking the spirits of the dead, it was because such spirits could, in fact, come; otherwise, his prohibition would have been needless. If they were able to come in his time, they still can today. And if they are spirits of the dead, then they are not demons exclusively. We must be logical above all.

Priest – The Church does not deny that good spirits can communicate, since it acknowledges that saints have manifested. But it cannot consider as good those who come in order to contradict its immutable principles. The Spirits teach of future punishment and reward, but they do not teach as the Church does; the Church alone can judge the spirits' teachings and distinguish the good from the evil.

A.K. – That is the big question. Galileo was accused of heresy and of being inspired by the Devil because he revealed a law of nature that proved the error of a belief regarded as unassailable; he was condemned and excommunicated. If the Spirits had concurred with the Church's exclusive point of view, and if they had not proclaimed freedom of conscience and condemned certain abuses, they would have been welcomed by the Church and would not have been regarded as demons.

This is also the reason why all religions – Islam as well as Catholicism – believe themselves to be in the exclusive possession of the absolute truth, and why they regard any doctrine that is not completely orthodox from their point of view as the work of the Devil. Now, the Spirits have not come to overthrow religion, but like Galileo, to reveal new laws of nature. If some points of faith are disputed because of this, it is because they are in conflict with these laws, as in the case of belief in the sun's movement. The issue is in knowing if an article of faith can annul a law of nature, which is the work of God. And if this law is acknowledged, wouldn't it be wiser to interpret dogma in light of it instead of attributing it to the Devil?

Priest – Let's leave the issue of demons; I know that it has been diversely interpreted by the theologians. The theory of reincarnation, on the other hand, seems more difficult to reconcile with dogma because it is nothing more than metempsychosis taken afresh from Pythagoras.

A.K. – Now is not the time to discuss an issue that would require a long explanation. You can find it discussed in *The Spirits' Book* and in *The Gospel according to Spiritism.*[25] I will say only a few words about it.

The metempsychosis of the ancients consisted in the transmigration of humans' souls into animals, which would imply degradation. Besides, this doctrine was not what is commonly believed. Transmigration into animals was not considered a condition inherent to the nature of the human soul, but as a temporary punishment; thus, the souls of murderers would pass into the bodies of savage beasts to receive their punishment therein; those of the unchaste, into swine and wild boar; those of the inconstant and inconsistent, into birds; those of the lazy and ignorant, into aquatic animals. After a few thousand of years, more or less, according to the culpability of this kind of prison, the soul would re-enter humanity. Animal reincarnation was therefore not an absolute condition, and we can see that it was allied with human reincarnation. The proof of it is that the punishment of timid men would consist in passing into the bodies of women to be exposed to scorn and insults.[26] It was a kind of bogeyman for the simple-minded, much more than an article of faith among philosophers. Just as one says to children: "If you are naughty, the wolf will eat you," the ancients said to criminals: "You will turn into wolves." Today they say: "The Devil will get you and carry you off to hell."

The plurality of existences, according to Spiritism, differs essentially from metempsychosis in that it does not accept the

---

[25] See *The Spirits' Book*, nos. 166 ff., ibid, 222 and 1010. Later titled *The Gospel according to Spiritism*, chaps. IV and VI. – Auth.

[26] See *La pluralité des existences de l'âme*, by Pezzani. – Auth.

incarnation of souls into animals, even as a punishment. The Spirits teach that the soul does not regress, but that it progresses continuously. Its different corporeal lives take place in humanity; each existence is a step forward on its path of intellectual and moral progress – which is quite different from metempsychosis. Not being able to acquire full development in one sole existence, frequently shortened by accidental causes, God allows it to use a new incarnation either to finish the task it was unable to finish or to start over what it had done badly. Expiation in the corporeal body consists of the tribulations one endures while in it.

As for the issue of knowing if the plurality of existences is or is not contrary to certain dogmas of the Church, I will limit myself to saying that one of two things is true: either reincarnation exists or it does not; if it does, it is within the laws of nature. In order to prove that it does not exist, we would have to prove that it is contrary not to dogma but to such laws, and that we can find another law that would explain more clearly and logically the questions that only reincarnation can solve.

Moreover, it is easy to demonstrate that certain dogmas find a rational endorsement in reincarnation that renders them acceptable to those who used to reject them because they did not understand them. So it's not a matter of destroying, but of interpreting. This will occur later by necessity. Those who will not accept the interpretation will be perfectly free, as they are today, to believe that it is the sun that revolves around the earth. The idea of the plurality of existences is becoming popularized with astonishing speed because of its sound logic and its conformity with God's justice. Once it is acknowledged as a natural truth and accepted by everyone, what will the Church do?

In sum, reincarnation is not a doctrine invented for the needs of a cause, nor is it a personal opinion. It either is or isn't a fact. *If it is demonstrated that there are certain things that are materially impossible without reincarnation, we must accept the fact that they are the result of reincarnation*, because if it is part of nature, it cannot be annulled by an opposing opinion.

Priest – According to spirits, are those who do not believe in them or their manifestations less fortunate in the next life?

A.K. – If this belief were indispensable for people's salvation, what would become of those who, since the world began, have not held it, and those who, for a long time to come, will die without holding it? Could God close the door of the future to them? No, the Spirits who teach us are more logical than that; they tell us: God is supremely just and good and does not make people's future destinies depend on conditions outside their will; they do not say: *Without Spiritism there is no salvation*, but like Christ: *Without charity there is no salvation.*

Priest – Then allow me to tell you that, since the Spirits teach only the principles of the morals we find in the Gospel, I do not see of what use Spiritism can be since we used to be able to be saved before it and we still can be without it. That would not be the case if the Spirits had come to teach some great new truths, some principles that would change the face of the world as Christ did. At least Christ did it by himself alone and his doctrine was unique, whereas there are spirits by the thousands who contradict each other; some say white; others, black. From this it follows that, from the beginning, their adherents have formed many sects. Wouldn't it be better to leave spirits alone and hold on to what we already have?

A.K. – You are mistaken, sir, not to abandon your point of view of taking the Church as the sole criterion of human knowledge. If Christ spoke the truth, Spiritism could not do otherwise; and instead of throwing stones at it, it should be welcomed as a powerful auxiliary that has come to confirm, through all the voices beyond the grave, the fundamental truths of religion that have been refuted by disbelief. For materialism to fight against Spiritism is understandable, but for the Church to unite with materialism against it is inconceivable. What is just as inconsistent is that the Church labels as demonic a teaching that is based on the same authority and proclaims the divine mission of the founder of Christianity.

But did Christ say all there was to say? Could he reveal everything? No, because he himself said: "I still have many things to tell you, but you would not understand them, which is why I speak to you in parables." Spiritism has come at this time – now that people are mature enough to understand it – to complete and explain what Christ touched upon only lightly, or spoke about only in allegorical form. Of course, you will say that the responsibility for this belongs to the Church. But to which one? To the Roman, Orthodox or Protestant Church? Since they are not in agreement, each one has given its own explanation and claimed this privilege. Which one has managed to unify all the dissident denominations? God is wise, and foreseeing that humans would get their passions and prejudices involved, he did not want to entrust them with the care of this new revelation. He entrusted it to spirits, his messengers, who have proclaimed it to every corner of the globe and apart from any particular denomination so that it could apply to all of them, and so that no one could turn it to his or her own advantage.

On the other hand, haven't the many Christian denominations turned away from the path traced out by Christ? Are his moral precepts scrupulously observed? Haven't his words been twisted to make them an argument for ambition and human passions when, in fact, they are a condemnation of them? Spiritism, on the other hand, through the voice of the Spirits sent by God, has come to call for the strict observation of his precepts by those who have turned away from them. Mightn't this last motive in particular be the one that qualifies it as the work of Satan?!

You are wrongly giving the name *sect* to a few differences of opinions related to spirit phenomena. For many, at the beginning of any science, when the observations are still incomplete, it isn't at all surprising that contradictory theories would arise; but such theories rest on details and not on the fundamental principle. *Schools* can thus explain certain facts in their own way, but these are no more sects than the different systems that divide our scholars regarding the exact sciences, such as in medicine, physics, etc. So delete the word sect because it is entirely inaccurate for the case in question. Moreover, hasn't Christianity given birth to a multitude of sects since its inception? Why hasn't the word of Christ been powerful enough to impose silence on every controversy? Why is it susceptible to interpretations that still divide Christians today into different churches, each claiming to be the sole keeper of the truth necessary for salvation, cordially detesting each other and denouncing each other in the name of their Divine Master, who preached only love and charity? Human weakness, will you say? So be it; how can you expect Spiritism to triumph suddenly over this weakness and transform humanity as though by magic?

Now, I will address the question of usefulness. You stated that Spiritism teaches us nothing new; that is an error. It teaches a great deal to those who do not stop at the surface. Moreover, had it done nothing more than to put the maxim: *Without charity there is no salvation*, which unites people, in the place of *Without the Church there is no salvation*, which divides them, that alone would have marked a new era for humankind.

You also stated that we could do without Spiritism. Agreed. Just like we could do without a multitude of scientific discoveries. People did just as well before the discovery of all the new planets; before eclipses were calculated; before the microscopic world was known about – and a hundred other things. In order to live and grow their wheat, peasants don't have to know what a comet is, and yet nobody denies that all these things have expanded the circle of ideas and have enabled us to penetrate deeper into the laws of nature. Well, the world of spirits is one such law, which Spiritism has enabled us to know by teaching us the influence it has on the corporeal world. Supposing that its usefulness were limited to just that, wouldn't the revelation of such a power be great enough?

Now, let's take a look at its moral influence. Let's say that it teaches absolutely nothing new in this respect. What is religion's greatest enemy? Materialism, because materialism believes in nothing; well, Spiritism is the negation of materialism, which has no more reason to exist. It is no longer by means of reasoning or blind faith that materialists are told that everything does not come to an end with their bodies, but by means of the phenomena, which are shown to them and which allow them to touch them with their fingers and see them with their eyes. Isn't that by itself lending a small service to humankind, to religion? But that isn't all: add the certainty of the future life, the living scenario of those who have gone before us, showing the need for the good and the inevitable consequences of evil. That is why, without being a religion per se, it essentially takes religious ideas and develops them in people who have none, and it strengthens them in those who are uncertain. Religion therefore finds a support in it, not for those persons with narrow minds, who see religion entirely in the doctrine of eternal fire and in form more than in essence, but for those who see it according to the grandeur and majesty of God.

In other words, Spiritism enlarges and elevates ideas, and it combats abuses produced by selfishness, cupidity and ambition. But who would dare defend them and declare themselves to be their champion? Although it is not indispensable to salvation, Spiritism facilitates it and sets us firmly on the path of the good. Moreover, what sensible person would dare assert that a lack of orthodoxy is more reprehensible in God's eyes than atheism and materialism? I pose the following questions outright to all those who fight Spiritism from the point of view of its religious consequences:

1. Who will be worse off in the future life: those who believe in nothing, or those who, believing in general truths, do not accept certain parts of Church dogma?

2. Will Protestants and schismatics be mixed in together in the same punishment as atheists and materialists?

3. Are those who are not orthodox in the strict sense of the word, but who do all the good they can, who are kind and indulgent toward their neighbors and honest in their social relationships, be less assured of their salvation than those who believe in everything, but who are hard, selfish and uncharitable?

4. Which is worth more in God's eyes: the practice of Christian virtues without the practice of the duties of orthodoxy, or the practice of the latter without the duties of morality?

So, Reverend, I have responded to the questions and objections that you have addressed to me; but as I told you at the beginning, without any preconceived intention of leading you to our way of thinking or of changing your convictions, I have restricted myself to enabling you to consider Spiritism from its true point of view. If you had not come to me, I would not have gone looking for you. That does not mean that we would scorn your adherence to our principles, if that had occurred – very far from it. On the contrary, we are happy for all the adherents we can attract, and who are all the more valuable to us when they come freely and willingly. Not only do we not have the right to exert any constraint over anyone, but we would hesitate to trouble the conscience of those who, having beliefs with which they are satisfied, do not willingly come to us.

We said that the best way to become enlightened about Spiritism is to study the theory first; the phenomena will then come naturally and you will understand them, regardless of the order in which they are brought up by the circumstances. Our publications are created with the goal of facilitating this study; consequently, that is the route we recommend.

The first reading should be this summary, which presents a collection of the most salient points of the science. By reading it, one can get an idea about it and be convinced that, in essence, it contains something very serious. In this short exposition, we have adhered to indicating points that should especially rivet the attention of the observer. Ignorance of the fundamental principles is the cause of erroneous appraisals by the majority of those who judge what they do not understand, or do so according to their preconceived ideas.

If this first contact has created a desire to know more about Spiritism, people should read *The Spirits' Book*, where the principles of the doctrine are fully developed; next, *The Mediums' Book* for the experimental part, meant to serve as a guide for those who want to proceed by themselves, and for those who want to get a clear idea of the phenomena. Then come the assorted works in which the applications and consequences of the doctrine are developed such as *The Gospel according to Spiritism*, *Heaven and Hell according to Spiritism*, etc.

The *Revue Spirite* is a sort of applications course due to the numerous examples and developments it contains on the theoretical and the experimental aspects.

To serious individuals who have done a preliminary study, it would be a pleasure for us to verbally provide the necessary explanations on the points they might not have entirely understood.

Chapter II

Elementary Notions of Spiritism

Elementary Notions of Spiritism

Preliminary Remarks

1. It would be a mistake to think that witnessing a few extraordinary phenomena would be enough for certain disbelievers to be convinced. Those who cannot believe in a soul or spirit in the human being cannot believe in it outside the human being either. Consequently, by denying the cause, they deny the effect. Hence, they nearly always come with a preconceived idea and a negative stance that keeps them from making a serious and impartial observation. They ask questions and raise objections to which it is impossible to immediately respond completely, because it would be necessary to give a sort of course and to start from the beginning for each individual. The result of prior study is that it can respond beforehand to objections, the majority of which are founded on the ignorance of the cause behind the phenomena and the conditions in which they are produced.

2. Those who are unfamiliar with Spiritism believe that spirit phenomena can be produced in the same way that other phenomena can be produced in physics and chemistry experiments. Hence, their intention to subject them to their will and their refusal to place themselves in the conditions needed to observe them. Since in principle they do not believe in the existence and intervention of spirits – at least they do not understand their nature or their modes of action – they act as if they were dealing with raw matter, and since they do not get what they were asking for, they conclude that there are no spirits after all.

If they would look at the issue from a different perspective, they would understand that spirits are human souls, that after death we ourselves will be spirits and that we too would be ill-disposed to serve as playthings to satisfy the fantasies of the curious.

3. Even though certain phenomena may be induced because they result from free intelligences, they are never at our complete disposal, no matter who we are, and whoever attempted to obtain them at will would be demonstrating either their ignorance or their bad faith. We must wait for the phenomena and understand them as they happen, and quite frequently it is at the moment when it is least expected that the most interesting and most conclusive incidents occur. Persons who seriously want to learn must therefore approach this subject – like all others – with patience and perseverance, and do everything that needs to be done; otherwise, they would be better off not to concern themselves with the matter.

4. Spiritist meetings meant for spirit manifestations do not always present the best conditions, whether for obtaining satisfactory results or for leading disbelievers to conviction; we must admit that there are meetings from which disbelievers leave less convinced than when they arrived, raising objections to those who talk to them about the serious nature of Spiritism by mentioning the often-ridiculous things they saw. They are no more logical than those who judge an art by the sketches of an apprentice, a person by his or her caricature, or a Greek tragedy by a parody on it. Spiritism has its students too, and persons who want to know more about it should not do so by drawing upon one sole source; only by examining and comparing can they arrive at a decision.

5. Frivolous meetings have grave consequences for beginners who attend them because they give them an erroneous idea of the character of Spiritism. Those who attend only meetings of this sort will never be able to take seriously something they see treated frivolously by the very persons who claim to be its adherents. Prior study will teach them to judge the importance of what they see and to separate the good from the bad.

6. The same line of reasoning applies to those who judge Spiritism by certain eccentric books that can give them only an incomplete and foolish idea of it. Authentic Spiritism is no more responsible for those who understand it badly or who practice it wrongly than poetry is responsible for those who write bad verse. It is deplorable that such works exist, they say, because they compromise the true science. Of course, it would be preferable for only good works to be available, but the greater error falls to those who do not go to the trouble to study the subject thoroughly. The same applies to all the arts and sciences. Even on the most serious subjects aren't there treatises that are absurd and packed full of errors? Why would Spiritism be any more privileged in this respect, especially at its beginning? If those who criticize it would stop judging it by its appearances, they would know what it accepts and what it rejects, and they would not accuse it of what it itself rejects in the name of reason and experience.

Concerning Spirits

7. Spirits are not, as often imagined, separate beings within creation. They are souls of those who used to live on the earth or on other worlds, stripped of their corporeal envelope. Whoever believes in the existence of the soul after the death of the body must therefore also believe in the existence of spirits. To deny spirits is to deny the soul.

8. Generally speaking, people have a mistaken idea about the make-up of spirits. They are not, as some believe, vague and indefinite

beings, nor are they flames like will-o'-the-wisps or ghosts like in the tales about souls from another world. They are beings like we are, with a body like ours, but fluidic and invisible in its normal state.

9. While the soul is united to the body during life, it possesses a two-fold envelope: one heavy, coarse and destructible, which is the body; the other fluidic, light and indestructible, called the *perispirit*.

10. Thus, in the human being there are three essential components: 1) the *soul* or *spirit*, which is the intelligent principle that harbors the thought, will and moral sense; 2) the *body*, which is the material envelope that enables the spirit to relate to the exterior world; and 3) the *perispirit*, which is the fluidic, light, imponderable envelope that serves as the connection and intermediary between the spirit and the body.

11. When the outer envelope is spent and can no longer function, it succumbs and the spirit rids itself of it like the fruit rids itself of its husk, the tree of its bark, the snake of its skin; in other words, as if it were taking off an old and useless garment. This is what is called *death*.

12. Death is nothing but the destruction of the material envelope; the soul abandons it like a butterfly leaving its chrysalis; however, it retains its fluidic body or perispirit.

13. The body's death frees the spirit from the envelope that had bound it to the earth and made it suffer; once freed of this burden, it possesses only its ethereal body, which allows it to travel space and traverse distances at the speed of thought.

14. The union of the soul, perispirit and physical body comprise the *human being*; the soul and perispirit apart from the body comprise the being called the *spirit*.

Note: The *soul* is thus a simple being; the *spirit*, a two-fold being and the *human being*, a three-fold being. Hence, it would be more precise to keep the word *soul* to designate the intelligent principle, and the word *spirit* to refer to the semi-material being formed from this principle plus the fluidic body. However, since one cannot conceive of the intelligent principle separate from all matter, or the perispirit not being animated by the intelligent principle, the terms *soul* and *spirit* are usually employed interchangeably. It is the appearance only that consists in taking the part for the whole, in the same way that one says that a town is populated by so many souls, or a settlement by so many houses. Philosophically, however, it is essential to differentiate between them.

15. Spirits clothed with physical bodies comprise humankind or the visible, corporeal world; when they are rid of these bodies, they make up the spirit or invisible world. They populate the space in the midst of which we live, without our even suspecting it, just as we used to live in the midst of the world of the infinitesimal without suspecting it before the microscope was invented.

16. Spirits are not, therefore, abstract, vague and indefinite beings, but concrete, circumscribed beings, who, if visible, would resemble humans; thus, it follows that, if at some given moment, the veil hiding them were to be lifted, they would form an entire population around us.

17. Spirits retain all the perceptions they had while on earth, but to a higher degree because their faculties are no longer deadened by matter. They experience sensations unknown to us; they see and hear things that our limited senses do not enable us to see or hear. For them there is no darkness, except for those whose punishment requires them to be in darkness temporarily. All our thoughts reverberate within them and they can read them like an open book. What we may be able to hide from a living person cannot be hidden once that person becomes a spirit.[27]

18. Spirits are everywhere: in our midst and at our side, rubbing elbows with us and observing us constantly. Due to their continued presence amongst us, spirits are the agents of diverse

---

[27] See *The Spirits' Book*, no. 237. – Auth.

phenomena; they perform an important role in our mental world and to a certain degree, in our physical world; consequently, they are one of the forces of nature.

19. Once the survival of the soul or spirit after death is accepted, it is reasonable to accept the survival of affectionate relationships; otherwise, the souls of our relatives and friends would be lost forever to us.

Since spirits can go everywhere, it is also reasonable to assume that those who used to love us during their life on earth continue to love us after death; that they can approach us, desiring to communicate with us by utilizing the means at their disposal. Experience has confirmed this fact.

In effect, experience has shown that spirits hold on to the serious relationships they had while on earth and that they take delight in coming to those whom they loved, especially when they are attracted by the affectionate thoughts and sentiments sent to them; on the other hand, they are indifferent toward those who show indifference toward them.

20. Spiritism's objective is to verify and study the manifestations of spirits, their faculties, their happy or unhappy conditions, and their future; in other words, to know about the spirit world. Because such manifestations have been confirmed, the result has been the irrefutable proof of the existence of the soul, its survival after the body and its individuality after death, i.e., the future life. Consequently, it is the negation of materialist doctrines, not only by means of reason but by the facts.

21. A more or less normal idea held by persons who are not familiar with Spiritism is the belief that spirits must know all things and possess supreme wisdom simply because they are free of matter. This is a serious mistake.

Since spirits are merely the souls of human beings, they do not suddenly reach perfection upon leaving their earthly envelope. The spirit's progress only occurs over time, and it is only successively that it gets rid of its imperfections and acquires the knowledge it lacks. It would also be illogical to believe that the spirit of a primitive or of a criminal could suddenly become wise and virtuous, just as it would be contrary to God's justice to believe that it would remain unevolved forever.

Since there are humans of all degrees of knowledge and ignorance, goodness and malice, the same applies to spirits. There are those who are only frivolous and playful; others who are deceitful, fraudulent, hypocritical, evil and vindictive, and still others who are possessed of sublime virtues and wisdom unknown upon the earth. Such diversity in the character of spirits is one of the most important points to consider because it explains the good or evil nature of the communications that may be received, and it is especially important to be able to distinguish between them.[28]

Communications with the Invisible World

22. Having accepted the existence, survival and individuality of the soul, Spiritism is left to answer one principal question: *Are communications between souls and the living possible?* This possibility is a result of experience. Once the exchange between the visible and invisible worlds has been established as a fact, and once the nature, cause and means of this exchange is understood, a whole new field opens up to observation and is the key to a multitude of problems; at the same time, it is a powerful moralizing element since it puts an end to any doubts regarding the future.

23. In many people's minds, what sheds doubt on the possibility of communicating with the dead is the mistaken idea regarding the state of the soul after death. The soul is

---

[28] See *The Spirits' Book*, no. 100: *The Spirit Hierarchy; The Mediums' Book*, chap. XXIV. – Auth.

usually imagined to be a breath, a vaporous being, or something vague that can only be understood by means of thought; or something that evaporates and goes off to who knows where, to such a far away place that it is hard to understand how it could return to the earth. If, to the contrary, we consider its union with a fluidic, semi-material body, with which it forms a physical, individual being, its communications with the living hold nothing incompatible with reason.

24. Since the visible world lives in the midst of the invisible world and is in constant contact with it, it follows that these two react incessantly upon each other; that, since there are human beings, there are spirits too, and that if the latter have the ability to manifest themselves, then they must have done so in all ages and amongst all cultures. However, as of late, spirit manifestations have increased substantially, and have taken on a greater character of authenticity. It was in the designs of Providence to put an end to the scourge of disbelief and materialism by means of obvious proofs, enabling those who have left the earth behind to come and attest to their existence, and to reveal their happy or unhappy condition to us.

25. The communications between the visible and invisible worlds may be secretive or open, spontaneous or induced.

Spirits act upon humans secretively through the thoughts they suggest to them and through certain influences; they act openly through effects discernible to the senses.

Spontaneous manifestations occur unexpectedly and fortuitously. Quite often, they occur to persons unfamiliar with Spiritist ideas, and who, for that very reason, cannot understand them; consequently, they attribute them to supernatural causes. Manifestations that are induced occur by means of certain individuals endowed with special faculties for producing such effects, and who are designated by the name *mediums*.

26. Spirits can manifest in many different ways: by means of sight, hearing, touch, noises, movements of objects, writing, drawing, music, etc.

27. Spirits sometimes manifest spontaneously through noises and raps, which are frequently their way of attesting to their presence and calling attention to themselves – just like someone knocking on a door to let those inside know someone is there. There are spirits who do not limit themselves to causing moderate noises, but who go so far as to produce a racket that sounds like dinnerware breaking, doors opening and closing, or furniture being overturned. Some even cause real trouble and damage.[29]

28. Although invisible to us in its normal state, the perispirit is ethereal matter, nonetheless. In certain cases, the spirit can undergo a sort of molecular modification that renders it visible and even tangible; this is how apparitions are produced. This phenomenon is no more extraordinary than steam, which is invisible when it is extremely rarified, but which becomes visible when it is condensed.

Spirits who make themselves visible nearly always appear as they did while alive so that they can be recognized.

29. The ongoing and widespread sighting of spirits is extremely rare, but isolated apparitions are quite frequent, especially at the time of death. The liberated spirit seems to be in a rush to see its relatives and friends again, as if to advise them that it has just left the earth and to tell them that it is still alive. Any person can delve into his or her memories and see how many authentic incidents of this type – unperceived at the time – have occurred not only at night during sleep, but in broad daylight while wide awake. Formerly, such incidents would have been considered supernatural and extraordinary, and attributed to magic and sorcery; today, disbelievers attribute them to imagination. However, since Spiritist science has provided the

---

[29] See *Revue Spirite*, 1858: *L'Esprit frappeur de Bergzabern*, pp. 125, 153, 184; ibid: *L'Esprit frappeur de Dibbelsdorf*, p. 219; ibid: 1860: *Le Boulanger de Dieppe*, p. 76; ibid: *Le fabricant de Saint Pétersbourg*, p. 115; ibid: *Le chiffonnier de la rue de Noyers*, p. 236. – Auth.

key to them, we know how they are produced and that they are not outside the order of natural phenomena.

30. It was with the help of its perispirit that the spirit used to act upon its physical body; it is with this same fluid that it continues to manifest itself by acting upon inert matter, producing noises and moving tables and other objects, which it lifts, knocks down or carries about. There is nothing surprising about this phenomenon if we consider the fact that the most powerful motors use the most rarified and even imponderable fluids such as air, steam or electricity.

It is also with the help of its perispirit that the spirit enables a medium to write, speak or draw. Not having a tangible body to act ostensibly when it wants to manifest, it uses the medium's body and borrows its organs, with which it acts as if it were its own body by means of the fluidic emanation it pours out over the medium.

31. It is by this same means that the spirit acts upon the table in the phenomenon known as the *turning* or *talking tables*, whether to cause them to move with no specific purpose in mind, or whether to produce intelligent raps to spell out the letters of the alphabet in order to form words and sentences. This is called *typtology*. In this phenomenon, the table is merely an instrument that the spirit uses in the same way that it uses a pencil in order to write. It endows the table with momentary life by means of the fluid that penetrates it; however, *the spirit does not become part of the table*. Emotional persons who see a being who used to be dear to them manifest and thus hug the table act foolishly because it is exactly as if they were hugging a baton that a friend was using to produce raps. The same applies to those who talk directly to the table as if the spirit were contained within the wood itself, or as if the wood had become the spirit.

When communications occur by this means, the spirit must be represented not as if it were within the table, but beside it, *with the same appearance it had when alive* and the way it would be seen at that moment if it could make itself visible. The same applies to written communications: the spirit should be thought of as being at the medium's side, guiding the hand or transmitting its thought via a fluidic current.

Whenever the table becomes detached from the floor and floats in the air without any means of support, the spirit does not lift it with its arms, but envelops it and penetrates it with a sort of fluidic atmosphere that neutralizes the effects of gravity, like the air in balloons and paper kites. This penetrating fluid momentarily gives the table a specifically greater lightness. When it is held to the floor, it is similar to what happens to the bell-jar from which all the air has been removed. All these comparisons are used only to demonstrate the similarity of the effects, not the complete similarity of the causes.

When the table chases someone, it is not the spirit who is doing the chasing, because it can remain peacefully in the same spot while moving the table by means of a fluidic current that enables it to move the table at will. When raps are heard within the table or somewhere else, the spirit is not beating it with its hand or with some other object; it is directing a jet of fluid that produces the effect of an electric-like jolt at the point where the noise is heard. It can change the noise, just as the sounds produced by the action of air can be changed.

Therefore, one can see that it is no more difficult for a spirit to *lift a person* than to lift a table, move an object from one place to another, or throw it about; these phenomena are produced according to one and the same law.

32. One can see by these few explanations that there is nothing supernatural or extraordinary about spirit manifestations. They are phenomena induced according to the law that governs the exchange between the visible and invisible worlds, a law as

natural as the law of electricity, gravity, etc. Spiritism is the science that enables us to know about this law, just as mechanics enables us to know about the law of motion, and optics, the law of light. Being part of nature, spirit manifestations have been produced in all ages; once understood, the law governing them explains a series of problems that used to be considered insolvable; it is the key to a multitude of phenomena exploited and amplified by superstition.

33. Once removed from the arena of the extraordinary, these phenomena are in no way repugnant to reason, because they may be placed alongside all other natural phenomena. In the ages of ignorance, all effects whose causes were not understood were regarded as supernatural. A string of scientific discoveries narrowed the circle of the extraordinary; the knowledge of this new law has reduced it to nothing. Therefore, those who accuse Spiritism of having resuscitated the extraordinary demonstrate that they are talking about something they know nothing about.

34. Spirit manifestations are of two types: *physical effects* and *intelligent effects.* The former are material and ostensive, such as movements, noises, the carrying of objects, etc.; the latter consist in the normal permutation of thought with the help of signs, words, and especially, writing.

35. Communications received from spirits may be good or bad, correct or erroneous, profound or superficial, depending on the nature of the spirits that manifest. Those that display wisdom and knowledge are spirits that have evolved; those that display ignorance and evil qualities are little-evolved spirits, but who will evolve with time.

Spirits can only respond to things they know about, according to their advancement, and furthermore, to things they are *allowed* to talk about because there are things they must not reveal, since it has not yet been given to humans to know about everything.

36. Due to the diversity in the qualities and aptitudes of spirits, it is not enough simply to address any spirit available in order to receive a correct response to every question, because, on many subjects, it can give only its personal opinion, which may be right or wrong. If it is wise, it will acknowledge its ignorance about what it does not know; if it is frivolous or deceitful, it will respond to anything without any concern for the truth whatsoever; if it is proud, it will offer its idea on the matter as if it were the absolute truth. This is why the book of 1 John 4:1 states: *Do not believe every spirit, but test the spirits to see if they are of God.* Experience has proven the wisdom of this advice. Thus, it would be imprudent and thoughtless to accept everything that comes from spirits without testing it first. That is why it is crucial to understand the nature of the spirits with whom we are relating.[30]

37. The quality of spirits may be determined by their language. The language of truly good, high order spirits is always dignified, noble, logical and lacking in contradictions; it displays wisdom, benevolence, modesty and the purest morality; it is concise and does not employ needless words. Regarding ignorant or proud low order spirits, the emptiness of their thoughts is almost always made up for by a superabundance of words. Every obviously erroneous thought, every maxim contrary to sound morality, every piece of foolish advice, every gross, trivial or just plain silly expression, and lastly, every trace of malevolence, presumptuousness or arrogance are incontestable signs of the spirit's unevolved character.

38. Low order spirits are ignorant to various degrees; their moral horizon is limited and their discernment restricted. They often have only an erroneous and incomplete idea of matters and are still under the influence of earthly preconceptions, which they sometimes assume to be true; thus, they are incapable of solving

---

[30] See *The Mediums' Book*, no. 267. – Auth.

certain issues. They can lead us intentionally or unintentionally into error concerning what they themselves do not understand.

39. All low order spirits are not, therefore, downright evil; there are those who are only ignorant and frivolous; others are facetious, witty or fun-loving spirits who know how to pull off a cunning, scathing joke. Moreover, we may find in the spirit world – just as on the earth – every sort of wickedness or every degree of intellectual and moral excellence.

40. High order spirits are concerned solely with intelligent manifestations intended for our instruction. Physical or purely material manifestations are most often assigned to low order spirits, who are commonly called *rapping spirits*, just as amongst us, feats of physical strength are performed by manual laborers and not scholars.

41. Communicating with spirits must always be done calmly and thoughtfully; we must never lose sight of the fact that spirits are the souls of men and women, and that it would be inappropriate to make them the object of a game or entertainment. If we owe due respect to mortal remains, we ought to have even more respect for the spirit. Frivolous and thoughtless meetings thus fail in their duty, and persons who take part in them should be mindful that they themselves may be called to the spirit world at any moment and would not look favorably on being treated with such little deference.

42. Another, equally important point to consider is the fact that spirits are free; they communicate when they want, with whom they want and when they are able because they have their occupations to attend to. They are not at the beck and call of anyone, no matter who they are, and no one has the right to make them come against their will or make them reveal what they must keep silent about. Consequently, no one can say for certain that a particular spirit will come upon being evoked at a set time, or respond to this or that question. To say otherwise is to display one's complete ignorance about the most basic principles of Spiritism. *Only charlatanism has failsafe sources.*

43. Spirits are attracted out of affinity, similarity of tastes and character, and the intention of whomever desires their presence. High order spirits would no more attend a pointless meeting than a scholar would attend a meeting of thoughtless children – plain common sense says it could not be otherwise. If they sometimes attend such meetings, it is for the purpose of providing healthy counsel, combating vice or trying to lead someone onto the right path. If they are not heeded, they withdraw. It would be completely wrong to think that serious spirits could possibly enjoy responding to futilities or idle questions that display neither respect for them nor any real desire to learn, and even less to think they would come to put on a show to entertain the curious. If they did not do such things during their lifetime, they would not do so after their death.

44. Frivolous meetings result in attracting frivolous spirits who are looking for nothing else but the opportunity to deceive and mystify. For the same reason that serious individuals do not attend inconsequential gatherings, serious spirits attend only serious meetings, whose purpose is instruction and not curiosity. These are the types of meetings in which high order spirits enjoy providing their teachings.

45. The result of what we have stated so far is that in order to be worthwhile every Spiritist meeting must be serious and reverential as the number one condition. Everything must occur respectfully, religiously and honorably if its aim is to obtain the habitual concourse of good spirits. It must not be forgotten that if these same spirits were present at such meetings while incarnate, they would have been given the respect to which they are even more entitled after death.

46. It is useless to allege that certain curious, frivolous or recreational experiments would convince disbelievers; actually, just the opposite is the case. Disbelievers who are already inclined to mock the most sacred beliefs cannot see something serious where entertainment is involved. They cannot be led to respect something that is not presented to them in a respectable manner; consequently, useless and frivolous meetings – those that display no order, seriousness or concentration, always leave a bad impression. What is most convincing, however, is the proof of the presence of those whose memory is dear to them. In light of their serious, solemn words and the intimate details they reveal, such disbelievers blanch and tremble with emotion. But because they have so much respect, admiration and fondness for the person whose soul appears to them, they feel shocked and scandalized to see him or her come to a disrespectful gathering in the midst of dancing tables and the comedic performances of thoughtless spirits. Disbelievers that they are, their minds reject such an alliance between the serious and the frivolous, the religious and the profane, and that is why they label the whole thing as trickery, and often leave even less convinced than when they came.

Meetings of this nature always do more harm than good because they keep more individuals away from the Doctrine than they lead to it, not to mention the fact that they open the way for detractors to find plenty of reasons to mock them.

47. It is a mistake to make a sport of physical manifestations; if such manifestations no longer carry the weight of a philosophical teaching, they nevertheless are useful from the phenomenological point of view because they represent the ABCs of the science, to which they have provided the key. Although they are not as useful as they once were, they still help to convince certain people. Even so, order and decency should not be excluded from meetings where experiments are performed. If such experiments were always performed appropriately, they would more easily convince disbelievers and would in every respect produce better results.

48. Some people have gotten a completely mistaken idea regarding evocations. There are those who believe they involve bringing back the dead with the morbid appearance of the grave. The little we have already stated so far should be enough to correct this error. Only in novels, ghost stories and plays are the discarnate dead seen to leave their graves dressed ridiculously in their burial shrouds and rattling their bones. Spiritism, which never performs miracles, has never produced anything of the sort and has never made a dead body come back to life; once the body is in the grave, it is there forever. But the fluidic, intelligent spirit being does not remain there wrapped in its coarse envelope; it disengages from it at the moment of death, and once the separation occurs, it has nothing more in common with it.

49. Malevolent criticism is pleased to represent spirit communications as involving the outlandish and superstitious practices of magic and necromancy. If those who speak of Spiritism without knowing anything about it had gone to the trouble of studying the subject, they would have spared themselves the trouble of wasting their imagination or making allegations that serve no other purpose than proving their ignorance and ill will. For the benefit of persons unfamiliar with the Spiritist science, we will state that there are neither days, times nor places that are more propitious than others for communicating with spirits; that neither formulas, sacramental or cabalistic words are needed to evoke them; that neither training nor initiation is needed; that no use of symbol or material object, whether to attract them or to repel them, is effective, and that thought alone is sufficient; and lastly, that mediums, without leaving their normal state, receive their communications as simply and as naturally as if they were dictated by incarnate persons. Only charlatanism could employ eccentric mannerisms and add ridiculous accessories.

Evoking spirits is done in God's name with respect and concentration: this is all that is recommended to serious persons who wish to communicate with serious spirits.

The Providential Aim of Spirit Manifestations

50. The providential aim of spirit manifestations is to convince disbelievers that all does not end for human beings when their life on earth ends, and to give believers a more correct idea regarding the future. Good spirits come to instruct us for our improvement and progress, but not to reveal to us what we must not yet know or what we must learn solely by our own efforts. If it were enough to simply ask spirits in order to get the solution to every scientific problem or to make discoveries or profitable inventions, any ignoramus could become a genius at no cost, and any lazy person could get rich without having to work for it – which is not what God has willed. Spirits help persons of genius through inspiration, but in order to leave the merit to them they do not exempt them from having to do work or research.

51. It would be completely wrong to see spirits as merely fortunetellers' helpers. Serious spirits refuse to concern themselves with useless matters. Frivolous, mocking spirits concern themselves with anything and everything, respond to anything and everything, and predict whatever people want them to predict with no concern at all for the truth; they feel a mischievous sense of pleasure in deceiving gullible persons. That is why it is essential to be perfectly certain about the nature of the questions that can be put to spirits.[31]

52. Apart from what can be of help to moral progress, there is nothing but uncertainty contained in revelations that may be

---

[31] See *The Mediums' Book,* no. 286: Questions that may be addressed to spirits. – Auth.

received from spirits. The first regrettable consequence for persons who divert their faculty from its providential aim is to be fooled by the deceitful spirits that swarm around people; the second is to fall under the control of these same spirits, who can, by way of false advice, lead them to real, material misfortune; the third is to lose after death the benefit of having known Spiritism.

53. Thus, manifestations are not meant to serve material interests; their usefulness lies in their moral consequences. However, if they led to no further results than to make known a new law of nature and to physically demonstrate the existence of the soul and its survival after death, they would accomplish much, because it would open up a broad new way to philosophy.

Concerning Mediums

54. Mediums display a wide variety in their aptitudes, which render them more suitable or less so for obtaining this or that phenomenon, or this or that type of communication. According to such aptitudes, we may say that there are *physical effects, intelligent communications, seeing, speaking, hearing, sensitive, drawing, polyglot, poetic, musical, writing, etc.* mediums. A medium cannot expect what is outside his or her faculty. Without understanding the various mediumistic aptitudes, the observer cannot be informed about certain difficulties or impossibilities that may be encountered in the practice of mediumship.[32]

55. Physical effects mediums are most particularly capable of inducing material phenomena, such as movements, raps, etc., with the aid of tables or other objects. When these phenomena express a thought or obey a will, they are intelligent effects, which for that very reason, point to an intelligent cause and are a way for spirits to

---

[32] See *The Mediums' Book*, chap. XVI, no. 185. – Auth.

manifest. By means of a number of ordinary raps, we may receive answers such as *yes* or *no,* or the designation of letters of the alphabet that may be used to form words or sentences. This primitive method is very slow and does not lend itself to lengthy exchanges. Talking tables began the science; nowadays, there are means of communication that are as fast and complete as the ones used between incarnates; tables serve only incidentally and for experimentation.

56. Of all the means of communication, writing is the simplest, fastest and most convenient, and allows the lengthiest exchanges; it is also the faculty most frequently found among mediums.

57. In order to obtain a written communication, physical intermediaries such as baskets, planchettes, etc. attached to a pencil were used at first.[33] It was later realized that such accessories were needless and that mediums could write directly with the hand as in ordinary circumstances.

58. Mediums write under the influence of the spirits who use them as their instruments; their hand is caused to write by involuntary movement, which most of the time they cannot control. Some mediums have no awareness of what they are writing; others are vaguely aware, although the thought is not their own. This is what distinguishes the *mechanical, intuitive* and *semi-mechanical mediums.* Spiritist science explains the way the spirit's thought is transmitted to the medium and the role the latter plays in communications.[34]

59. Mediums possess the faculty of communication, but effective communication depends on the will of spirits. If spirits do not want to manifest, mediums obtain nothing and are like instruments without musicians.

Spirits communicate only when they want to or when they are able to, and are not at anyone's beck and call; *no medium has the ability to make them come whenever desired and against their will.*

---

[33] See *The Mediums' Book,* chap. XIII, nos. 152 ff. – Auth.

[34] See *The Mediums' Book,* chap. XV, nos. 179 ff.; chap. XIX, nos. 223 ff. – Auth.

This explains the intermittence of the faculty in the best mediums, in addition to its suspension, which they sometimes must bear for several months.

Consequently, it would be erroneous to liken mediumship to a *talent*. Talents are acquired by work, and those who possess them are always master over them; mediums are never master of their faculty, because it depends on an outside will.

60. Physical effects mediums who on a regular basis and at their pleasure are able to obtain certain phenomena – if it does not involve trickery – are being used by low order spirits who enjoy putting on such exhibitions and who were perhaps involved in the same type of work when they were alive. Nevertheless, it would be absurd to believe that even such low order spirits would enjoy being put on display.

61. The darkness required for the production of certain *physical* effects of course arouses suspicion, but proves nothing against their reality. In chemistry it is a known fact that there are combinations that cannot occur under light, and that compositions and decompositions occur under the action of the luminous fluid. Since all spirit phenomena result from the combination of the personal fluids of both the spirit and the medium, and since these fluids are physical, it should come as no surprise that in certain cases the luminous fluid works against their combination.

62. Intelligent communications also occur by means of the fluidic action of the spirit upon the medium; the fluid of the latter must identify with the fluid of the former. The ease of the communication depends on the degree of *affinity* between the two fluids. Each medium is thus capable of receiving the *impression* or *impulse* of this or that spirit's thought to varying degrees. Such a medium may be a good instrument for one, but a bad instrument for another. The result is that even though two equally well-endowed mediums may be right next to each other, a spirit may manifest through one and not the other.

63. Therefore, it is a mistake to believe that it is enough simply to be a medium in order to receive communications from every spirit with the same ease. There are no more universal mediums for making evocations than there is a universal aptitude for inducing every type of phenomenon. Spirits prefer to look for instruments who vibrate in unison with them; if they were to impose themselves on the first to come along, it would be like forcing a pianist to play the violin, under the reasoning that if he or she knows music, he or she should be able to play every instrument.

64. Without harmony – the only quality that can lead to fluidic assimilation – communications are impossible, incomplete or false. They may be false because, in the absence of the spirit desired, there is no lack of others who are ready and willing to take advantage of the occasion to manifest, and who care very little about telling the truth.

65. The fluidic assimilation is at times completely impossible between certain spirits and mediums. At other times – and this is the most common case – it is only established gradually over time. This is what explains why spirits who are accustomed to manifesting through one particular medium do so more easily and why the first manifestations nearly always display a certain restraint and are less explicit.

66. Fluidic assimilation is as necessary in communications involving *typtology* as it is in those involving writing, since in either case there is a transmission of the spirit's thought, whatever the material means employed.

67. Since mediums cannot impose themselves on the spirit they want to evoke, it behooves the spirit itself to choose its own instrument. In any case, the medium must identify beforehand with the spirit through concentration and prayer, at least for a few minutes, and even for a few days, if possible, in order to induce and activate the fluidic assimilation. This is the way to attenuate the difficulty.

68. Whenever the fluidic conditions are not proper for the spirit to communicate directly with the medium, the communication may occur through the intermediary of the latter's spirit guide. In this case, the thought only arrives second hand; that is, after having passed through two sources. Thus, one can understand how important it is for the medium to be well assisted because if he or she is assisted by an obsessor, ignorant or proud spirit, the communication will inevitably be altered.

Here, the medium's personal qualities truly perform an important role due to the nature of the spirits he or she attracts. The most unworthy mediums can possess powerful faculties, but the safest are those who combine such strength with the best affinities in the spirit world. Now, these affinities are *in no way guaranteed* by the impressive names that spirits might use or that they might take when signing communications, but by the *consistently good* nature of the communications obtained from them.

69. Whatever the mode of communication may be, the practice of Spiritism from the experimental point of view entails many difficulties and is not without its problems for anyone who lacks the necessary experience. Whether one is experimenting for oneself or whether simply observing, it is crucial to know how to distinguish amongst the various natures of the spirits that can manifest, to know the causes of all the phenomena, the conditions in which they may be produced, and the obstacles that may be encountered, in order not to ask the impossible. And it is no less necessary to know about all the conditions and all the dangers of mediumship, the influence of the environment, moral dispositions, etc.[35]

---

[35] See *The Mediums' Book*, pt. 2. – Auth.

Dangers Mediums Might Encounter

70. One of the greatest dangers regarding mediumship is *obsession,* i.e. the control that certain spirits may have over mediums by imposing themselves on them with apocryphal names and by keeping them from communicating with other spirits. This is also a danger to the new and inexperienced observer, who, not being familiar with the characteristics of the phenomenon, may be fooled by appearances, like those who, not knowing medicine, may be mistaken about the cause and nature of a sickness. If prior study in this case is useful for observers, it is indispensable for mediums because it furnishes them the means of preventing a problem that could have regrettable consequences. That is why we feel that it is never too much to recommend studying before delving into the practice.[36]

71. Obsession presents three main, well-characterized degrees: *simple obsession, fascination* and *subjugation.* In the first, mediums are perfectly aware that they are not receiving anything good and they are not mistaken about the nature of the spirits who insist on manifesting through them, and from whom they would love to disentangle themselves. This sort of case is not all that serious: it is only a mere inconvenience and the medium can get rid of it by not writing for a while. When the spirit tires of not being listened to, it leaves.

Obsessive fascination is much more serious in that the mediums are completely deluded. Spirits who control them gain their trust to the point of paralyzing their judgment in analyzing their communications and making them believe that the most absurd things are truly sublime.

The distinctive characteristics of this type of obsession is that of causing mediums to be excessively susceptible; to believe that only

---

[36] See *The Mediums' Book,* chap. XXIII. – Auth.

what they themselves write is good, just and true, rejecting and even regarding as evil all critical advice and every critical observation; to break off relations with their friends rather than admit that they have been deceived; to envy other mediums whose communications are deemed better than theirs; to want to control Spiritist meetings, which they leave if they cannot prevail. They end up suffering such overwhelming domination that the spirit can compel them to assume the most foolish and compromising attitudes.

72. One of the distinctive characteristics of evil spirits is that they impose themselves; they give orders and expect to be obeyed. Good spirits never impose themselves; they provide counsel and if they are not heeded, they withdraw. As a result, evil spirits leave a feeling that is grueling and tiring and which produces a sort of uneasiness; it frequently causes a feverish agitation, and brusque, irregular movements. Good spirits, on the other hand, leave a calming and gentle feeling that instills a sense of true well-being.

73. *Obsessive subjugation,* which used to be called *possession,* is a physical coercion exerted by spirits of the worst kind and it can even neutralize the obsessee's free will. It is often limited to simple disagreeable feelings, but sometimes it causes disorderly movements, foolish actions, screams or incoherent or offensive words. The mediums subject to it are at times aware of their ridiculous behavior but they can do nothing about it. This state differs essentially from *pathological insanity,* with which it is wrongly confused, because in obsessive subjugation there is no organic lesion; since the cause is different, the curative measures must also be different. Applying the standard procedures of douches[37] and physical treatments to obsessive subjugation may often induce true insanity where there was nothing but a strictly moral cause to begin with.

---

[37] Hydrotherapy was widely used in the treatment of nervous and mental diseases in the 1800s. – Tr.

74. In insanity per se, the cause of the problem is internal and it is necessary to try to reestablish the organism to its normal state. In *subjugation*, the cause is external and it is necessary to rid the patient of an invisible enemy by opposing it not with medications but with *a moral power superior to its own*. Experience has shown that, in such a case, exorcisms have never produced a satisfactory result; they aggravate rather than improve the situation. By pointing out the true cause of the problem, only Spiritism can provide the means of combating it. The obsessor spirit must be educated morally, somehow; by means of wisely directed counsel, one can render it better morally and make it willingly renounce its torment of the patient, who is then liberated.[38]

75. As a rule, obsessive subjugation is individual; however, when a phalanx of evil spirits invades a population, subjugations can take on an epidemic scale. One such phenomenon occurred at the time of Christ; only a powerful moral superiority could have dominated those malevolent beings called *demons* and reinstate their victims' peace of mind.[39]

76. An important fact to consider is that obsession, whatever its nature, is independent of mediumship and may be found in every degree – especially the third kind – in a large number of individuals who have never even heard of Spiritism. In fact, since spirits have existed in every age, they must have exerted the same influence in every age. Mediumship is not a cause but only a means of manifesting such influence; hence, one can state with certainty that every obsessed medium must be enduring, in some way and frequently in the commonest acts of life, the effects of this influence, and that apart from mediumship it would express itself through other effects often attributed to those mysterious

---

[38] See *The Mediums' Book*, no. 279; *Revue Spirite*, Feb., Mar. and June of 1864: *La jeune obsédée de Marmande*. – Auth.

[39] Another such epidemic harangued a village in Haute-Savoie for several years. (See *Revue Spirite*, Apr. and Dec. of 1862; Jan., Feb., Apr. and May of 1863: *Les possédés de Morzines*. – Auth.

illnesses that escape every investigation by medicine. By means of mediumship, the malfeasant being betrays its presence; without mediumship, it is a hidden enemy no one suspects.

77. Persons who cannot believe in anything apart from matter cannot believe in a hidden cause, but when science finally emerges from its materialistic impasse, it will recognize, in the action of the invisible world that surrounds us and in the midst of which we live, a force that acts upon physical things as well as mental things. This will be the opening of a new road to progress and will provide the key to a multitude of wrongly understood phenomena.

78. Since obsession can never be caused by a good spirit, one essential point is that of knowing how to recognize the nature of the spirits who manifest. Unenlightened mediums can be deceived by appearances, whereas those who are prudent look out for the smallest signs of suspicion, and the spirit ends up withdrawing upon realizing there is nothing it can do. Prior understanding of the means of distinguishing between good and evil spirits is thus indispensable to mediums who do not want to expose themselves to being caught in a trap. It is no less indispensable to mere observers, who can thereby evaluate the worth of what they see and hear.[40]

Characteristics of Mediums

79. The mediumistic faculty is connected with the organism; it is independent of the medium's moral qualities and may be found in the most unworthy as well as in the most worthy individuals. This does not apply to the preference that good spirits give to the medium, however.

80. Good spirits communicate voluntarily to varying degrees through this or that medium according to their affinity with

---

[40] See *The Mediums' Book*, chap. XXIV. – Auth.

the medium's own spirit. What comprises the characteristics of mediums is not the ease with which they receive communications, but their ability to receive only good ones and not to become playthings of frivolous and deceitful spirits.

81. Mediums who leave much to be desired from the moral point of view sometimes receive very good communications, which can only have come from good spirits, and it would be a mistake to be surprised by this fact; it is often in these mediums' best interest and to give them wise advice. If they do not take advantage of it, they have only themselves to blame because they write their own condemnation. God, whose goodness is infinite, cannot refuse assistance to those who have the most need of it. The virtuous missionary who teaches good morals to criminals is acting in the same way as good spirits do with imperfect mediums.

Furthermore, when good spirits want to provide a useful, widespread teaching, they will make use of the instrument at hand; however, they will leave him or her when they find one with whom they have more affinity and who will take advantage of their lessons. When good spirits withdraw, low order ones, unconcerned about moral qualities, then have an open playing field.

The result is that morally imperfect mediums who do not mend their ways sooner or later become prey to evil spirits, who quite often lead them to their ruin and great misfortune, even while in this world. As for their faculty, as beautiful as it was and would have remained, it becomes tarnished first by being forsaken by good spirits and then by being lost altogether.

82. Even the most deserving mediums are not exempt from manifestations by deceitful spirits; first, because none are sufficiently perfect not to have a weak spot that can provide access to evil spirits; second, in order to exercise their judgment, good spirits at times allow it to happen so that their mediums can learn how to tell truth from error and be wary so as not to accept anything blindly without having tested it first. But deception does not come from good spirits and any respectable name that signs an error is necessarily apocryphal.

This may also be a test of patience and perseverance for any Spiritist, medium or not. Those who become discouraged by a few deceptions show good spirits that the latter cannot count on them.

83. It is no more surprising to see evil spirits obsess respectable persons than it is surprising to see evil persons persecuting good people.

It is interesting that, ever since *The Mediums' Book* was published, obsessed mediums have become much less numerous, because, having been forewarned, they are on their guard and watch for the smallest signs that may betray the presence of a deceitful spirit. Most of the ones who are obsessed either did not study the subject first or did not heed the counsels offered to them.

84. What comprises a medium per se is the mediumistic faculty, which may be more developed or less so; what comprises the *sure* medium, the one who can truly be classified as a *good medium*, is the use of the faculty, the aptitude to serve as an interpreter for good spirits. Regardless of the faculty, a medium's ability to attract good spirits and repel evil ones is due to his or her moral ascendancy. This ascendancy is in proportion to the sum of the characteristics that make such mediums moral persons, and with it they obtain the affinity of good spirits and exert control over evil ones.

85. For the same reason, the sum of mediums' moral imperfections liken them more to the nature of evil spirits and keep them from the ascendancy needed to avoid them. *Instead of being the ones who exert control over evil spirits, evil spirits exert control over them.* This applies not only to mediums, but to everyone else, since there is no one who is not influenced by spirits. (See nos. 74, 75 above)

86. In order to impose themselves on mediums, evil spirits know how to skillfully exploit all their moral defects; the one that gives them the greatest access is *pride*, the sentiment that dominates most obsessed mediums, especially those who are *fascinated*. Pride leads them to believe in their infallibility and to scorn advice. Unfortunately, this sentiment is encouraged by the praise of which they might be the object; when their faculty is a little transcendental, they are sought out and flattered; they end up believing in their own importance and regard themselves as indispensable, which leads them to their downfall.

87. While imperfect mediums pride themselves with the illustrious names – usually apocryphal – that sign the communications they receive, and regard themselves as the privileged interpreters of heavenly powers, *good mediums* never feel sufficiently worthy of such a favor and always maintain a healthy distrust of the quality of what they receive; that is, they do not trust their own judgment. Since they are only passive instruments, they understand that if the communication is good, they cannot regard it as their personal merit any more than they can be held responsible if it is bad. It would be foolish to believe unquestionably in the identity of the spirits who manifest through them, and they leave the matter to be judged by disinterested third parties without any more offence to their personal vanity for an unfavorable judgment than an actor would be for criticism leveled at the play in which he or she played a part. Their distinctive character displays simplicity and modesty; they are happy with the faculties they possess, not out of vanity but rather as a means of being useful, which they willingly are when the occasion arises, and without being offended if they are not given top preference.

Mediums are spirits' intermediaries and interpreters; thus, it is the responsibility of the evoker, or even the mere observer, to determine the worthiness of the instrument.

88. The mediumistic faculty is a gift from God as are all faculties that may be used for either good or evil, and it may be abused. Its purpose is to put us in direct communication with the souls of those who used to live so that we may receive their teachings and be initiated into the future life. Just as sight puts us in communication with the visible world, mediumship puts us in communication with the invisible one. Those who employ it for useful purposes, for their own and their neighbors' advancement, are fulfilling a true mission, for which they will be rewarded. On the other hand, those who abuse it and use it on useless matters or for material gain divert it from its providential aim and must sooner or later bear the consequences like anyone else who makes bad use of a faculty.

Charlatanism

89. Certain spirit manifestations lend themselves quite easily to being imitated, but even though they may be exploited like so many other phenomena by means of trickery and sleight-of-hand, it would be absurd to conclude that they do not actually exist at all. For anyone who has studied and knows the normal conditions under which they may be produced, it is easy to tell an imitation from an authentic manifestation. Furthermore, an imitation could never be complete and could deceive only unknowing observers incapable of understanding the characteristic nuances of authentic phenomena.

90. The manifestations easiest to imitate are certain physical effects and common intelligent effects, such as movements, raps, apportations, direct writing, banal responses, etc. The same does not apply to intelligent communications of a high level. To imitate the former, only skillfulness is required; to simulate the latter, an uncommon erudition, exceptional intellectual abilities and a comprehensively broad – so to speak – faculty of improvisation would be necessary.

91. Persons who are unfamiliar with Spiritism may be led to suspect the good faith of mediums; study and experience provide them the means of assuring themselves of the authenticity of the phenomena. Additionally, the best guarantee lies in the medium's absolute disinterest and honorability. There are persons who, because of their position and character, are beyond any suspicion. If the possibility of material gain can encourage fraud, common sense would indicate that where there is nothing to gain, charlatanism has nothing to do.[41]

92. We may find both enthusiasts and eccentrics among Spiritism's adherents – as in everything else. They are usually the worst propagators because the ease with which they accept everything without an in-depth examination arouses distrust. Knowledgeable Spiritists are on their guard against blinding enthusiasm and observe everything coolly and calmly. This is the way not to fall victim to either illusions or deceptions. Besides the issue of good faith, beginning observers should, before anything else, take into consideration the seriousness of the character of the persons they address.

The Identity of Spirits

93. Since all the defects of humanity may be found among spirits, cunningness and deceitfulness may also be found. There are spirits who have no qualms about adorning themselves with the most respectable names in order to inspire trust. Hence, it is necessary to refrain from believing wholeheartedly in the authenticity of every signature.

---

[41] See *The Mediums' Book*, chap. XXVIII on Charlatanism and Trickery, Mediums for Hire, Fraudulent Manifestations; *Revue Spirite*, 1862, p. 52. - Auth.

94. Identity is one of the big problems of practical Spiritism and it is often impossible to prove its authenticity, especially when dealing with highly evolved spirits from ancient times. Amongst those that manifest, many do not have names that mean anything to us; consequently, to provide us with something to fix our thoughts on, they may take the name of a known spirit of the same category. Thus, if a spirit communicates using the name St. Peter, for example, that does not mean that it really is the apostle himself; it could be him, or it could be a spirit of the same order, who has been sent by him.

The question of identity in this case is by all means secondary, and it would be childish to connect any importance to it; what matters is the nature of the teaching. Is it good or bad, worthy or unworthy of the personage who took the name? Would he or she approve of it or condemn it? That is the whole issue.

95. Identity is easiest to prove when dealing with contemporary spirits, whose character and habits are known, because it is by the habits and characteristics of their private lives that their identity is more assuredly revealed, and often in an incontestable manner. Whenever relatives or friends are evoked, it is their personality that is of most interest and it is thus quite natural to try to prove their identity. However, for those who are only partially familiar with Spiritism, the means to do so are generally insufficient and may lead to error.

96. A spirit can reveal its identity through a multitude of circumstances highlighted in its communications, which reflect its habits, character, language and even its familiar quirks. It may also reveal its identity through intimate details, which it *willingly* divulges to persons it cares about – these are the best proofs. However, it is very rare that it will satisfy any direct questions asked of it in this regard, especially if asked by persons who are indifferent toward it, and whose sole objective is curiosity or proof. The spirit proves its identity as it wishes or as it is able according to the type of its interpreter's faculty, and often these proofs are super-abundant. The mistake is to want it to provide them in the way the evoker wants them given; that is, when it refuses to yield to his or her demands.[42]

Contradictions

97. The contradictions that often appear in what spirits say should come as a surprise only to observers who merely possess an incomplete understanding of the Spiritist science. Contradictions result from the nature of the spirits themselves, who, as already stated, can only understand matters according to how evolved they are; many of them know even less than certain incarnates. Regarding a multitude of facts, they can provide only their personal opinion, which may be correct to some degree while still reflecting the earthly prejudices they have not yet abandoned. Others fabricate their own theories about what they do not yet understand, particularly regarding scientific matters and the origin of things. Consequently, it should come as no surprise that they are not always in agreement with one another.

98. We may be surprised at finding contradictory communications signed by the same name. According to the circumstances, only low order spirits could differ in what they say, because high order spirits never contradict one another. Whoever is relatively inexperienced regarding the mysteries of the spirit world should understand the ease with which certain spirits adorn themselves with borrowed names in order to make what they say more believable. Thus, we may safely conclude that if two communications that are radically contradictory *as to the depth of the thought* carry the same respectable name, one of the two is necessarily apocryphal.

---

[42] See *The Mediums' Book*, chap. XXIV: The Identity of Spirits; *Revue Spirite*, 1862, p. 82: *Fait d'identité*. – Auth.

99. Two ways may serve to settle our thoughts concerning issues of doubtful identity: the first is to submit communications to the severe test of reason, common sense and logic. This is the recommendation given by all good spirits, but one that is discouraged by deceitful spirits, who know very well that they can only lose with a serious examination. That is why they avoid discussion and want to be blindly believed.

The second criterion of true identity lies in the agreement of the teaching. When the same principle is taught in several places by different spirits and mediums who do not know each other and who are not under the same influence, we can conclude that it entails more truth than one coming from only one source and which contradicts the majority.[43]

The Consequences of Spiritism

100. In light of the uncertainty concerning revelations made by spirits, one might ask: So what good is the study of Spiritism, after all?

It is useful to materially prove the existence of the spirit world.

Since the spirit world is composed of the souls of those who used to live on the earth, it proves the soul's existence and its survival of the body.

The souls who manifest reveal their joys and their sufferings according to the way their earthly life was lived, which thus proves the notion of future rewards and punishments.

As souls or spirits describe their state and their situation, they correct erroneous ideas made regarding the future life, and especially the nature and duration of punishments.

---

43 See *The Mediums' Book*, chap. XXVII: Contradictions and Deceptions; *Revue Spirite*, Apr. 1864, p. 99; *The Gospel According to Spiritism: Introduction*, pt. II, Authority of the Spiritist Doctrine. – Auth.

Consequently, the future life goes from being a vague and uncertain theory to being a consummate and positive fact, which results in the need to labor as much as possible during our short, present life on behalf of our everlasting future life.

Let us imagine that a 20-year-old man is certain that he will die at 25. What will he do during those five years? Will he labor for the future? Surely not. He will make every effort to enjoy himself to the utmost and would think it wrong to impose meaningless fatigue and privation on himself. However, if he is certain that he is going to live to be 80, he will act otherwise because he will understand the need to sacrifice a few moments of repose in the present to ensure repose in the future for several years. The same would be the case for anyone for whom the future life is an uncertainty.

Doubt about the future life naturally leads people to yield completely to the pleasures of the present; hence the excessive importance given to material wealth.

The importance given to material wealth arouses covetousness, envy and jealousy in those who have little vis-à-vis those who have much. From covetousness to the desire to obtain at any cost what their neighbor possesses, there is only one small step; hence the hatred, disputes, lawsuits, wars and all the ills engendered by selfishness.

With doubt about the future, people who are oppressed during this life by sadness and misfortune see death as the only end to their suffering. Hoping for nothing more, they think it is rational to shorten it through suicide.

Without hope in the future, it is quite natural for people to be affected and become desperate from the disappointments they experience. The violent jolts they feel as a result resonate in their minds, the cause of most cases of insanity.

Without the future life, the present one is of crucial importance to people, the sole object of their concerns, and they relate everything to it. That is why they want at any price to enjoy not only material wealth but honors; they aspire to stand out, to rise above others and to eclipse their neighbor by means of ostentation and status; hence the unbridled ambition and importance they give to titles and all the futilities of self-centeredness, for which they would sacrifice even their honor because they see nothing else beyond it.

Certainty about the future life and its consequences completely changes the order of people's ideas and enables them to see matters from a different perspective; the veil is lifted and they discover an immense and splendid horizon. In light of the infinite and the grandeur of the life beyond the grave, the present life vanishes like a second before the centuries, like a grain of sand before the mountain. Thus, everything else becomes small and petty, and they marvel at the importance once given to matters so ephemeral and childish; hence, in the events of life, a calm tranquility appears, which is already happiness in comparison to the worries and torments people impose on themselves when trying to rise above others; the same applies for vicissitudes and disappointments, to which they become indifferent. By removing any hint of despair, it prevents numerous cases of insanity and diverts the thought from suicide. With certainty about the future, individuals can hope and resign themselves; with doubt about it, they lose patience because they expect nothing beyond the present.

From the examples of those who used to live, people are shown that the sum of future happiness is the result of the moral progress achieved and the good that has been done while on earth; that the sum of future unhappiness is the result of the sum of the vices and bad deeds; consequently, in all those who are well convinced of this truth, there is a wholly natural inclination to do good and avoid evil.

When the majority of people are imbued with this idea, when they profess these principles and practice the good, the result will be that the good will win out over evil in this world; that people will no longer seek to harm one another; that they will govern their social institutions for the good of all and not for the privilege of the few; in other words, they will understand that the law of charity taught by Christ is the fount of happiness even while in this world, and they will base their civil laws on the law of charity.

The awareness of the spirit world that surrounds us and its action upon the corporeal world reveals one of the powers of nature, and consequently the key to a multitude of incomprehensible phenomena both in the physical and mental realms.

Once science recognizes this new power, unknown to it even today, it will correct a multitude of errors that have arisen from attributing everything to one sole cause: matter. The acknowledgement of this new cause in nature's phenomena will be a lever for progress and will produce the effect of discovering an entirely new agent. With the help of Spiritist law, science's horizon will broaden, just as it broadened with the help of the law of gravity.

Once scholars from atop their cathedras start proclaiming the existence of the spirit world and its actions on life's phenomena, they will instill in our youth the counterweight to materialist ideas, instead of predisposing them to denying the future.

In their lessons on classical philosophy, professors teach the existence of the soul and its attributes according to the various schools of thought, but without any material proof. Isn't it strange that now that such proofs have appeared, they are rejected and regarded as superstitious by these same professors? Aren't they telling their students: We teach you the existence of the soul, but there is nothing that proves it? When a scholar transmits a theory on a scientific matter, he or she zealously seeks and happily gathers all the data that may prove the theory true. So, how could a professor of philosophy, whose duty it is to prove to his or her students that they have a soul, regard with disdain the means of providing them with a patent demonstration?

101. Let us say that spirits are incapable of teaching us anything that we don't already know or that we cannot find out about by ourselves; even then, the mere proof of the spirit world's existence should be enough to bring about a revolution in thought. Now, a revolution in thought necessarily leads to a revolution in the order of things, and it is this revolution that Spiritism is preparing.

102. But spirits have done more than this. If their revelations are surrounded by certain problems and demand detailed precautions for them to be verified precisely, it is no less true that enlightened spirits – when we know how to question them and when they are permitted – can reveal unknown facts to us, provide us with explanations of incomprehensible things and place us on a more rapid path of progress. It is in this, especially, that the complete and careful study of the Spiritist science is indispensable in order not to ask of it what it cannot give; overstepping its bounds is what exposes us to being deceived.

103. The smallest causes can produce the largest effects; thus it is that, from a small seed arises a huge tree; that the fall of an apple leads to the discovery of the law that governs worlds; that frogs twitching on a plate revealed the galvanic force; it was also thus that, from the ordinary phenomenon of the turning tables arose proof of the invisible world, and from such proof a doctrine that in just a few years has crossed the world and can regenerate it simply by providing evidence for the reality of the future life.

104. In conformance with the axiom that there is nothing new under the sun, Spiritism teaches little in way of absolutely new truths. There are no absolute truths except those that are eternal; since they are founded upon the laws of nature, such truths, taught by Spiritism, have therefore existed throughout all ages. There, we can find the seeds that a more complete study and more careful observation have developed further. The truths taught by Spiritism are thus consequences rather than discoveries.

Spiritism has neither discovered nor invented spirits, nor has it discovered the spirit world, which has been believed in throughout all ages; it has only demonstrated it by means of physical phenomena and has shown it in its true light, thereby freeing it from the prejudices and superstitious ideas that have engendered doubt and disbelief.

Comment: Although incomplete, these explanations are enough to show the basis upon which Spiritism rests, the character of the manifestations, and the degree of trust that they may inspire according to the circumstances.

Chapter III

The Solution to a Few Problems by Means of the Spiritist Doctrine

The Solution to a Few Problems by Means of the Spiritist Doctrine

The Plurality of Worlds

105. *Are the many worlds traveling through space peopled with inhabitants as is the earth?*

All the Spirits have affirmed it and reason states that it must be so. Since the earth occupies no special class in the universe, either because of its position or size, there is nothing that would justify believing that it alone is privileged enough to be inhabited. Moreover, God could not have created those billions of globes simply for the pleasure of our own eyes, especially since the vast majority is beyond our sight.[44]

106. *If other worlds are inhabited, are all their inhabitants similar to those of the earth? In other words, could these inhabitants live amongst us and us amongst them?*

Their overall form might be more or less the same, but their composition must be adapted to the environment in which they live, just as fish are made to live in the water and birds in the air. If the environment is different – as everything would lead us to believe, and just as astronomical observations seem to show – their

---

[44] See *The Spirits Book*, no. 55; *Revue Spirite*, 1858, p. 65: *Pluralité de mondes*, by Flammarion. – Auth.

physical composition must be different also; hence, in their normal state they probably could not live amongst one another with the same bodies. All the Spirits have confirmed this to be a fact.

107. *Assuming that these worlds are inhabited, are they in the same position as the earth from the moral and intellectual point of view?*

According to what the Spirits have taught, the various worlds are at very different degrees of evolution; some are in the same condition as the earth; others are even less evolved: the human beings on them are even more brutish, more physical and more inclined toward evil. On the other hand, there are worlds on which human beings are morally, intellectually and physically more-evolved, where moral evil is unknown, where the arts and sciences have attained a degree of perfection incomprehensible to us, and where the inhabitants' less physical composition is subject neither to suffering, disease, nor infirmity. People live in peace without trying to harm one another, and they do not experience the vexations, troubles, afflictions or needs that assail earth's people. Moreover, there are worlds that are more evolved still, where the nearly fluidic corporeal envelope approaches more and more the nature of the angels. In the progressive series of the worlds, the earth is neither in the first nor the last category, but it is one of the most material and least evolved.[45]

The Soul

108. *Where is the seat of the soul?*

The soul is not, as is generally believed, located in any one part of the body. Along with the perispirit, it forms a fluidic, penetrable whole assimilating the entire body, with which it comprises a complex being and from which death is no more than a sort of *split*. One may visualize two like bodies interpenetrating

---

[45] See *Revue Spirite*, 1858, pp. 67, 108 and 223; ibid, 1860, pp. 318 and 320; *The Gospel according to Spiritism*, chap. III . – Auth.

each other, joined during life and separated after death. In death, one is destroyed while the other remains.

During life, the soul acts more specially upon the organs of thought and sentiment. It is simultaneously internal and external; that is, it radiates outward. It can even leave the body, travel far and manifest its presence somewhere else, as observation and somnambulistic phenomena have shown.

109. *Is the soul created at the same time as the body or before?*

Apart from the existence of the soul, this question is one of the most crucial, because its solution leads to the most important consequences. It is the only key to a multitude of problems unsolvable until now for lack of being considered.

There are two possibilities: either the soul exists or does not exist before the body's formation – there can be no middle ground. With the preexistence of the soul, everything is explained logically and naturally; without it, it is even impossible to justify certain dogmas of the Church. It is this very impossibility of justification that has led so many thinking people to disbelief.

The Spirits have resolved the question in the affirmative, and neither the phenomena nor logic can leave any doubt about it. However, once we accept the soul's preexistence as a simple hypothesis at least, we will see that most difficulties disappear.

110. *If the soul exists prior to the body, then before its union with the body did it possess its individuality and self-awareness?*

Without individuality and self-awareness, the results would be the same, as if it had not existed in the first place.

111. *Prior to its union with the body, had the soul achieved any progress or had it been stationary?*

The fact of the soul's prior progress is both the consequence of observation of the phenomena and the Spirits' teachings.

112. *Did God create all souls morally and intellectually equal or did God create some more perfect and intelligent than others?*

If God had created some souls more perfect than others, such favoritism would not be compatible with God's justice. Since all are God's creatures, why would God exempt some from labor while imposing it on others in order to achieve eternal happiness? The inequality of souls at their origin would be a negation of God's justice.

113. *If all souls are created equal, how can the diversity of aptitudes and natural predisposition amongst earth's humankind be explained?*

This diversity is the consequence of the progress the soul accomplished before its union with the body. Souls more advanced in intelligence and morality are those who lived longer and progressed more prior to their incarnation.

114. *What is the state of the soul at its origin?*

Souls are created simple and ignorant, that is, without knowledge or an understanding of good and evil, but with an equal aptitude for all things. At their beginning, they are in a sort of infancy with neither their own will nor perfect awareness of their existence. Little by little, their free will develops along with their ideas.[46]

115. *Did the soul accomplish its previous progress in the soul state per se, or in a previous corporeal existence?*

Besides the Spirits' teachings regarding this point, the study of the differing degrees of humans' advancement on the earth demonstrates that the soul's previous progress must have been accomplished over a series of corporeal existences that varied in number according to the degree they have reached. Such deduction is the result of having observed the phenomena occurring before our eyes every day.[47]

---

[46] See *The Spirits' Book*, nos. 114 ff. – Auth.

[47] See *The Spirits' Book*, nos. 166-222; *Revue Spirite*, Apr. 1862, pp. 97-106. – Auth.

Human Beings during their Life on Earth

116. *At what moment does the union between the soul and body occur?*

At conception, the spirit, although still in the errant state, becomes connected by a fluidic tie to the body with which it is to unite. This tie tightens as the body develops. From then on, the spirit is overcome by a sort of confusion that continues to increase. At the time of birth, this confusion is complete and the spirit loses its self-awareness; it regains its ideas gradually, starting at the moment of the child's first breath. At this point, the union is complete and definitive.

117. *What is the intellectual state of the child's soul at the moment of its birth?*

The soul's intellectual and moral state is the same as before its union with the body; that is, the soul possesses all the ideas it had acquired previously, but due to the confusion that accompanies its change, its ideas are momentarily in a latent state. They gradually awaken, but manifest only in proportion to the development of the child's organs.

118. *What is the origin of innate ideas, precocious dispositions, and instinctive aptitudes for an art or science without having undergone any formal instruction?*

Innate ideas can have only two possible sources: the creation of some souls more perfect than others, in which case they would have been created at the same time as the body, or the previous progress accomplished prior to the union between the soul and the body. Since the former is incompatible with God's justice, that leaves only the latter. Innate ideas are the result of knowledge acquired during previous existences, and which remain in a state of intuition to serve as the basis for acquiring new ideas.

119. *How can geniuses appear in social classes deprived of any intellectual education?*

This fact shows that innate ideas are independent of the environment in which people are educated. Both environment and education develop innate ideas, but they do not provide them. Persons of genius are incarnations of already-advanced spirits, who have already progressed significantly. Thus, education may provide the instruction they still lack, but it cannot provide genius where there is none.

120. *Why are there children who are instinctively good in a wicked environment and in spite of bad examples, whereas others are instinctively evil in a good environment and in spite of good counsels?*

It is the result of already-accomplished moral progress, just as innate ideas are the result of intellectual progress.

121. *Of two children of the same parents and educated under the same conditions, why may one be intelligent and the other slow, one good and the other evil? Why is it that the child of a person of genius is sometimes a dullard and the child of a dullard a person of genius?*

This fact finds its support in the origin of innate ideas. Moreover, it shows that the soul of such a child in no way proceeds from the parents; otherwise, in virtue of the saying that the part is of the same nature as the whole, the parents would transmit their qualities and defects to their children, just as they transmit the principle of their corporeal qualities. In procreation, only the body proceeds from the body, whereas the souls are independent of one another.

122. *If souls are independent of one another, where does the mutual love of parents for their children come from?*

Spirits are brought together out of affinity, and birth into this or that family does not happen by chance. Most often it depends on the choice of the spirit who rejoins those whom it used to love in the spirit world or during previous lifetimes. Furthermore, parents have the mission to aid the progress of the spirits who incarnate in their children; and to encourage them, God inspires them to mutual affection; however, they often fail at their mission and are punished as a result.[48]

123. *Why are there bad parents and bad children?*

They are spirits who are brought together as a family not out of affinity, but as a trial, and often as a punishment for what they were in a previous existence. One parent is given a bad child because he himself or she herself was perhaps a bad child; in order to undergo the punishment of talion, the child is given a bad parent because he or she was a bad parent.[49]

124. *Why do we find certain persons born into a lowly condition possessed of instincts of dignity and greatness, while others, born into the upper classes, display instincts of a lower nature?*

This is an example of an intuitive memory of their character and the social position they occupied in a previous existence.

125. *What is the cause of the sympathies and antipathies between persons who meet for the first time?*

They are most often persons who once knew and perhaps loved each other in a previous existence, and who, upon meeting once again, are attracted to each other.

Instinctive antipathies also result from previous relationships.

These two sentiments may have a different cause, however. The perispirit radiates around the body a type of atmosphere imbued with the good or bad qualities of the incarnate spirit. By means of the contact of their spiritual fluids, two persons who meet experience the resultant feeling, which may be either pleasant or unpleasant. Their spiritual fluids tend either to intermingle or to repel each other according to their similar or dissimilar nature.

This is how the phenomenon of thought transmission may be explained. Through the contact of their spiritual fluids, two

---

[48] See *The Spirits' Book*, no. 379 on Childhood. – Auth.

[49] See *Revue Spirite*, 1861, p. 270: *La peine du talion*. – Auth. (See also *Heaven and Hell*, pt. 2, chap. VIII: Antoine B. – Tr).

souls understand each other somehow. They are in tune with each other and comprehend each other without even speaking.

126. *Why don't people remember their previous lives? Wouldn't such remembrance be necessary for their future progress?*

(See "Forgetfulness of the Past" – Dialogue with Visitor, above)

127. *What is the origin of the sentiment called the conscience?*

It is the intuitive remembrance of the progress accomplished in previous lives and of resolutions made by the spirit before incarnation – resolutions it does not always have the strength to keep once incarnated.

128. *Do human beings have free will or are they subject to fatalism?*

If their conduct were subject to fatalism, they would have no responsibility for the evil or merit for the good they do; hence, any punishment would be unjust and any recompense senseless. Humans' free will is a consequence of God's justice, the attribute that gives them their dignity and lifts them above all other creatures. This is so very true that the esteem they have for one another is due to their free will. Those who lose it accidentally because of sickness, insanity, chemical dependency or mental impairment are pitied or treated with contempt.

Materialism, which makes all the moral and intellectual faculties depend on the physical body, reduces humans to the status of being machines without free will, and consequently, with no responsibility for the evil or merit for the good they do.[50]

129. *Did God create evil?*

God did not create evil but established laws, and these laws are always good because God is supremely good. Those who obeyed them faithfully would be perfectly happy. But since spirits have free will, they do not always obey them; evil is the result of their breaking these laws.

---

[50] See *Revue Spirite*, 1861, p. 76: *La tête de Garibaldi*, ibid, 1862, p. 97: *Phrénologie spiritualiste*. – Auth.

130. *Are humans born good or evil?*

One must distinguish between the soul and the person. The soul is created simple and ignorant, meaning neither good nor evil, but because of its free will it is susceptible to taking either the good path or the evil one; in other words, to obeying or breaking God's laws. The person is born either good or evil according to whether he or she is the incarnation of an evolved or unevolved spirit.

131. *What is the origin of good and evil on the earth, and why is there more evil than good?*

The origin of evil on the earth is the result of the imperfection of the spirits incarnated on it. Because the earth is a less evolved world, the predominance of evil derives from the fact that most of the spirits that inhabit it are themselves less evolved or have progressed little. On more highly evolved worlds, where only purified spirits are allowed to incarnate, evil is either nearly or completely unknown.

132. *What is the cause of the ills that afflict humankind?*

The earth may be considered as both a world of instruction for little-evolved spirits and one of expiation for guilty spirits. Humankind's ills are the consequence of the moral imperfection of incarnate spirits. Through the contact of their vices, they make themselves mutually unhappy and punish one another.

133. *Why do bad individuals frequently prosper while good ones are the target of all sorts of afflictions?*

For those who see nothing but the present life and who believe it is the only one, this fact must seem a supreme injustice. This is not the case, however, when one considers the plurality of existences and the brevity of each when compared to eternity. The study of Spiritism shows that the prosperity of bad people has awful consequences for them in subsequent existences; that the afflictions of individuals of the good are, on the contrary, followed by a great and lasting happiness if they have borne their afflictions with resignation; for them, it is like one unfortunate day in a lifetime of prosperity.

134. *Why are some born into destitution and others into opulence? Why are there persons born blind, hearing and speech-impaired or afflicted with incurable diseases, whereas others have every physical advantage imaginable? Is this an effect of chance or of Providence?*

If it is an effect of chance, it cannot be one of Providence; if it is the effect of Providence, people might ask: where is God's goodness and justice? Clearly, it is because they do not understand the cause behind such ills that many are led to blame God. It is understandable that those who become poverty-ridden or infirm due to their imprudence or their excesses should be punished wherein they have sinned; however, if *the soul is created at the same time as the body*, what has it done to deserve such afflictions *from birth* or to be exempt from them? If we acknowledge the justice of God, we must acknowledge that these effects have a cause; if this cause does not lie in this life, it must lie in a previous one because in all things *the cause must precede the effect.* Hence, the soul must have lived before and it must have deserved the expiation. Spiritist studies have, in fact, shown us that more than one person born into poverty was once rich and respected in a previous existence, but made bad use of the wealth that God enabled him or her to administer; that more than one person born into abjectness was once proud and powerful; that quite often those who commanded with harshness are submitted to the mistreatment and humiliation that they forced others to bear.

A life of pain is not always one of expiation; it is quite often a trial chosen by the spirit itself, who sees it as a way to evolve more rapidly if it bears it with courage. Wealth is also a trial more perilous than poverty due to the temptations and abuses it arouses. The examples of those who have lived also show that it is a trial from which few manage to emerge victorious.

Differences in social positions would be all the more unjust – when they do not result from our conduct in the present life – if they didn't have a means of compensation. It is the conviction of that truth, acquired through Spiritism, which gives us the strength to endure life's vicissitudes and to accept our lot without envying the lot of others.

135. *Why are there severely mentally impaired persons?*

Their situation would hardly be at all reconcilable with God's justice if the theory of a single existence were true. No matter how miserable the situations individuals are born into may be, they can rise above them by means of intelligence and labor; mentally impaired persons, however, are destined from birth to death to suffer brutality and contempt.[51] There is no possible compensation for them. So, why would their soul have been created that way?

Spiritist studies of the mentally impaired have shown that their soul is as intelligent as the souls of the unimpaired; that such infirmity is an expiation inflicted on spirits for having abused their intelligence in a previous life, and that they suffer cruelly by feeling imprisoned by bonds they cannot break and by the contempt to which they are subjected, when they may have been lauded for their intelligence in a previous existence.

136. *What state is the soul in during sleep?*

During sleep, only the body rests; the spirit does not sleep. Experiments have shown that during this time the spirit enjoys its complete freedom and the full use of its faculties. It takes advantage of the body's rest and the times in which its presence is not needed in order to act freely and go wherever it wishes. During its lifetime,

---

[51] These were usually the circumstances at the writing of this book in 1859. – Tr. (This IS still true here and everywhere, probably less so in more advanced countries. Most severely mentally impaired people are segregated. You may want to mention that due to scientific research and the growth of societal values, severely mentally people (like that physicist on a wheel chair) is acknowledged and respected worldwide)

no matter how far it may travel from the body, the spirit remains connected to it by a fluidic tie that serves to call it back whenever its presence in the body is needed. This tie is broken only by death.

137. *What causes dreams?*

Dreams result from the spirit's freedom during sleep and are sometimes the remembrance of places and persons the spirit has seen or visited while in that state.[52]

138. *Where do presentiments come from?*

They are the spirit's vague and intuitive memories of what it learned during times of freedom; sometimes, they are secret warnings given by benevolent spirits.

139. *Why are there both primitive and civilized people?*

Apart from the preexistence of the soul, this question would be insolvable, unless we were to believe that God created primitive and civilized souls, which would be a denial of his justice. Furthermore, reason refuses to believe that, after death, the soul of the primitive either remains forever in its little-evolved state or that it is in the same position as the soul of the enlightened individual.

If one accepts the idea that there is one starting point for all souls – the only doctrine compatible with God's justice – the simultaneous presence of primitivism and civilization is a material fact that demonstrates the progress that some have achieved and that others are capable of achieving. The primitive's soul thus will attain the level of the civilized soul with time. However, since primitives die every day, their souls cannot attain such a level except through subsequent incarnations more and more perfected and suitable for their advancement, and after going through all the intermediary levels between the two extremes.

---

[52] See *The Spirits' Book:* The emancipation of the soul, sleep, dreams, somnambulism, second sight, lethargy, etc., nos. 400 ff.; *The Mediums' Book:* Evocations of living persons, no. 284; *Revue Spirite,* 1860, p. II: *L'Esprit d'un côté et le corps de l'autre;* ibid, 1860, p. 81: *Etude sur l'Esprit des personnes vivantes.* – Auth.

140. *Would it be possible, according to some people's way of thinking, that the soul incarnates only once but then goes on to accomplish further progress in the spirit state or in other realms?*

This proposition would be acceptable if on the earth there were only people of the same moral and intellectual level, in which case we could say that the earth is meant for only one specific level; the exact opposite seems obvious, however. In fact, it would be incomprehensible that primitives could not become civilized on earth, since there are many advanced souls incarnated on the same globe. From this we must conclude that the possibility for the plurality of earthly existences results from the very examples we have right before our eyes. If it were otherwise, we would have to explain: First, why would only earth have the monopoly on incarnation? Second, if such a monopoly were a fact, then why are there souls incarnated at every level of advancement?

141. *In the midst of civilized societies, why are there individuals of a level of ferociousness similar to the most barbaric primitives?*

They are little-evolved spirits who have left their former barbaric cultures to reincarnate in an environment unfamiliar to them, and in which they feel out of place, just as a boor would feel if suddenly brought into the environment of high society.

> Comment: It would be hard to believe, without denying God's justice and goodness, that the soul of a hardened criminal could have the same point of departure in this life as an individual full of every virtue. If the soul were not previous to the body, the soul of the criminal would be as new as the soul of the moral individual; why then would one be good and the other evil?

142. *Where do the distinctive characteristics of the various cultures come from?*

From spirits who share more or less the same tastes and inclinations and who incarnate in a sympathetic environment – and often in the same environment – where they can satisfy such inclinations.

143. *How do cultures progress and decay?*

If the soul were created at the same time as the body, the humans of today would be as new and as primitive as the humans of the Middle Ages. But why, then, are their habits more benign and their minds more developed? If in the death of the body the soul leaves the earth for good, we must ask further: What would be the result of the work done to improve a culture if it had to be recommenced with the new souls arriving each and every day?

Spirits incarnate into a sympathetic environment and according to the level of their advancement. For example, a person in one culture, who has progressed sufficiently but who did not find in that culture an environment corresponding to the level he or she has reached, will incarnate in a more advanced culture. As a generation moves a step forward, through sympathy it attracts new arrivals of more advanced spirits who perhaps might have previously lived in that same country and progressed. It is thus that, step by step, a nation advances. If the majority of the new arrivals were of a less evolved nature, and if the former inhabitants departing every day did not then return to a worse environment, the culture would decay and end up dying out.

> Comment: Such questions give rise to others which find their solution in the same principle; for example, where does the diversity of cultures on earth come from? Are there cultures that rebel against progress? Is the black race capable of attaining the level of the European?[53] Is slavery[54] useful to the progress of less evolved cultures? How can the transformation of humankind take place?[55]

---

[53] Kardec asks this question in the context of Europe's colonization of Africa in the 1800s, at the time this book was written. – Tr.

[54] See *The Spirits' Book*, no. 829: "Every instance of subjection of one human being to another is contrary to the law of God. Slavery is an abuse of power and will disappear with progress little by little, as will all other abuses." (See also nos. 830-832, ibid, on this subject.) *The Spirits' Book* was published in 1857 while slavery was still legally practiced in many parts of the world, including the United States. Unfortunately, other "severe forms of trafficking in persons" continue in our times, as attested by the U.S. State Department annual report "Trafficking in Persons." – Tr.

[55] See *The Spirits' Book:* The Law of Progress, nos. 776 ff.; *Revue Spirite*, 1862, p.1: *Doctrine des anges déchus*, ibid, 1862, p. 97: *Perfectibilité de la race nègre.* – Auth.

Human Beings after Death

144. *How does the soul's separation from the body occur? Does it occur suddenly or gradually?* The soul's liberation occurs gradually and at varying degrees of slowness according to individuals and the circumstances of their deaths. The bonds that used to unite the soul to the body are broken only little by little; the separation occurs less quickly if the person's life was more materialistic and sensually inclined.[56]

145. *What is the soul's situation immediately after the death of the body? Is it instantly aware of itself? In other words, what does it see? What does it feel?*

At the moment of death, at first everything is confused. The soul needs some time to get a hold of itself. It is dazed and in the state of someone awakening from a deep sleep, trying to understand his or her situation. As the influence of the matter from which it has just freed itself wears off, and the sort of fog that obscures its thoughts dissipates, the lucidity of ideas and the memory of its past return.

The duration of this state of confusion varies greatly; it may last only a few hours or several days, months or even years. It is shorter for those who during life identified with their future state because they immediately understand their situation; it is longer for those who lived more materialistically.

The sensations that the soul feels at this time also vary greatly. The confusion following death is not at all painful for morally upright persons; it is calm and in every way resembles the sensation that accompanies a peaceful awakening. For those whose conscience is not clean and who are more bound to the corporeal than the spiritual life, it is full of anxiety and distress, which increase as they regain their self-awareness. They are overcome with fear and a sort of dread at what they see, and especially of what they foresee.

---

56 See *The Spirits' Book*, no. 155. – Auth.

The sensation that may be termed physical is one of great relief and immense well-being; the spirit feels relieved of a burden and very happy at no longer feeling the corporeal pain experienced a few moments before; at feeling free, liberated, detached and alert, as if it had been freed from heavy chains.

In its new situation, the soul sees and hears what it saw and heard before death, but it also sees and hears other things that are beyond the coarse bodily organs. It experiences sensations and perceptions unknown to us.[57]

> Comment: These responses, as well as all those having to do with the soul's situation after death or during life, are not the result of a theory or system but of direct studies of thousands of individuals observed in every phase and period of their spirit existence, from the lowest to the highest degree of the hierarchy, and according to their habits during their earthly life, the kind of death, etc. When speaking of the spirit life, it is often stated that no one knows what happens there because no one has ever returned from it. That is a mistake because it is precisely those who are there who have come to instruct us, and God is allowing it more nowadays than ever before as a final warning to disbelief and materialism.

146. *After the soul has left the body, does it see God?*

The soul's perceptive faculties are proportional to its purification; only highly purified souls may enjoy God's presence.

147. *If God is everywhere, why can't all spirits see him?*

God is everywhere because God radiates everywhere, and one could say that the universe is immersed in divinity, just as we ourselves are immersed in the sun's light. But less evolved spirits are surrounded by a sort of fog that hides it from their eyes, and which dissipates only as they purify and dematerialize themselves. From the visual point of view, low order spirits are, in relation to God, like incarnates in relation to spirits: truly blind.

---

[57] See *Revue Spirite*, 1859, p. 224: *Mort d'un spirite*; ibid, 1860, p. 332: *Le réveil de l'Esprit*; ibid, 1862, p. 129 and 171: *Osèques de M. Sanson.* – Auth.

148. *After death, is the soul aware of its individuality? What evidence is there and how can we prove it?*

If souls did not retain their individuality after death, it would be both for them and for us as if they did not exist at all, and the moral consequences would be exactly the same. They would have no distinctive characteristics and criminals would be on the same level as morally upright individuals, which would mean that no one would have any interest in doing good.

In mediumistic manifestations, the soul's individuality is disclosed in a material manner, so to speak, by the language and qualities characteristic to each soul. Since they all think and act differently, some are good and others evil, some learned and others ignorant, some want what others do not; this is obvious proof that they are not merged into a homogenous whole. This goes without mentioning the obvious proofs they have provided us of having animated this or that particular individual while on earth. Thanks to experimental Spiritism, proof of the soul's individuality is no longer a vague concept but a result of observation.

The soul itself proves its individuality because its own thoughts and will are distinct from those of others. It also proves it by means of its fluidic envelope or perispirit, a sort of limited body that makes it a separate being.

> Comment: Some people think they can escape the criticism of materialism by believing in a universal intelligent principle, a portion of which we absorb at birth and which comprises the soul, and which we give back after death to the common mass, into which our souls blend like drops of water in the ocean. This theory – a sort of transition – does not deserve the name *spiritualism*, because it is as hopeless as materialism. The common reservoir of the Universal Whole would be the same as nothingness since there would be no more individualities there.

149. *Does the kind of death influence the state of the soul?*

The state of the soul varies considerably according to the

kind of death, but especially according to the nature of its habits during its earthly life. In natural death, the disengagement occurs gradually and without shock, and frequently begins even before the body's life is extinguished. In violent death through suicide, capital punishment or accident, the ties are broken all of a sudden; surprised by this occurrence, it becomes greatly confused by the change that has taken place in itself and cannot comprehend its situation. One fairly constant phenomenon in such cases is that the spirit is not convinced that death has occurred, and this delusion can last several months or years. While in this state, it comes and goes, looking after its affairs as if it were still in this world, but it is very perplexed when no one responds when it speaks. This delusion does not apply exclusively to violent deaths, however; it may be found in many individuals whose life was absorbed by materialistic pleasures and interests.[58]

150. *Where does the spirit go after having left the body?*

It does not become lost in the immensity of the infinite as is generally believed. It is in the errant[59] state in the spirit world, and most frequently it finds itself amongst those it used to know, and especially amongst those it used to love, as it is able to travel instantly over great distances.

151. *Does the soul retain its affections from earth?*

It retains all of its moral affections; it forgets only the material affections that are no longer important to it. That is why it joyously comes to see its relatives and friends once again, and is happy that they have remembered it.[60]

152. *Does the soul retain any memory of what it did while on the earth? Is it still interested in the endeavors it left unfinished?*

---

[58] See *The Spirits' Book*, no. 165; *Revue Spirite*, 1858, p. 166: *Le suicidé de la Samaritaine*; ibid, 1858, p. 326: *Un esprit au convoi de son corps*; ibid, 1859, p. 184: *Le Zouave de Magenta*; ibid, 1859, p. 319: *Un Esprit qui ne se croit pas mort*; ibid, 1863, p. 97: François Simon Louvet. – Auth.

[59] See *The Spirits' Book*, no. 224. – Tr.

[60] See *Revue Spirite*, 1860, p. 202: *Les amis ne nous oublient pas dans l'autre monde*; II - ibid, 1862, p. 132. – Auth.

That depends on how evolved it is and the nature of its endeavors. Dematerialized spirits care little about material matters and are happy to be free of them. As for the endeavors they had begun, according to their importance and usefulness, they sometimes inspire others with the thought of finishing them.

153. *In the spirit world, does the soul once again meet the relatives and friends who preceded it?*

Not only does it meet them, but it also meets many others it used to know in its previous existences. Usually, those for whom it held the most affection come to welcome it on its return to the spirit world, and they help it free itself from its earthly bonds. However, being denied meeting their loved ones once again is sometimes a punishment for guilty spirits.

154. *In the other life, what is the intellectual and moral state of children who died at a very young age? Are their faculties still as child-like as they were while incarnate?* The incomplete development of the organs of such children did not enable their spirits to manifest completely; once freed from their envelope, their faculties are as they were prior to incarnating. Since their spirits spent only a few moments physically alive, their faculties could not have changed.

> Comment: In spirit communications, the spirit of a child can therefore speak as that of an adult because it could be a highly advanced spirit. If it sometimes assumes child-like language, it does so in order not to deprive its mother of the enchantment of a fragile, delicate being adorned with all the grace of innocence.[61]

> The same question may be asked regarding the intellectual state of the souls of mentally impaired and insane persons after death; the answer lies in the aforementioned.

155. *After death, what is the difference between the souls of learned individuals and unlearned ones, and between the souls of primitives and civilized persons?*

---

[61] See *Revue Spirite*, 1858, p. 17: *Mère! Je suis là!* – Auth.

Approximately the same difference as between them during life, for entering the spirit world does not endow the soul with all the knowledge it lacked while on the earth.

156. *Do souls progress intellectually and morally after death?*

They progress more or less so, according to their will; some progress significantly, but they need to put into practice during the corporeal life what they have acquired in knowledge and morality. Souls who remain stationary return to an existence similar to the one they left, whereas those who have progressed merit an incarnation of a higher level.

Since progress is proportional to the spirit's will, there are spirits who for a long time retain the tastes and inclinations they had during life, and who pursue the same ideas.[62]

157. *Is a person's fate in the future life irrevocably sealed after death?*

The irrevocable sealing of a person's fate after death would be a complete negation of God's goodness and justice because there are many who did not depend on their own efforts to educate themselves sufficiently – not to mention mentally impaired and primitive individuals, and the countless children who die before having experienced life. Even among educated persons there are many who might think they are sufficiently perfected to be exempt from doing anything more; but is this not manifest proof that God gives of his goodness, allowing a person to do the next day what he or she did not do the day before? If fate is irrevocably sealed, why do people die at such differing ages, and why does not God, out of divine justice, allow everyone time to do the best possible or to repair the evil they have done? How can one be sure that a blameworthy person who died at thirty years of age would not have repented and have become a moral person if he or she had lived to be

---

[62] See *Revue Spirite*, 1858, p. 82: *La reine d'Oude*; ibid, p. 145: *L'Esprit et les héritiers*; ibid, p. 186: *Le tambour de la Bérésina*; ibid, 1859: p. 344: *Un ancien charretier*; ibid, 1860, p. 325: *Progrès des Esprits*; ibid, 1861, p. 126: *Progrès d'un Esprit pervers.* – Auth.

sixty? Why would God deny him or her such an opportunity when God gives it to others? By itself, the fact of the diversity of life's duration and the moral state of most people proves the impossibility – if one believes in God's justice – that the soul's fate is irrevocably sealed after death.

158. *In the future life, what is the fate of children who died at a very young age?*

This question is one of those that best demonstrates the justice and need of the plurality of existences. A soul who lived only a few moments and did neither good nor evil would merit neither reward nor punishment. According to Christ's maxim that *all are rewarded or punished according to their deeds*, it would be both illogical and contrary to God's justice to believe that, without having worked for it, such a soul would be called to enjoy the perfect bliss of the angels, or that it could be deprived of such; *nevertheless, it must have some kind of fate.* A combination of the two throughout eternity would also be an injustice. An existence interrupted at its beginning cannot thus have any consequences for the soul. Its current fate is the result of what it deserved from its previous existence; its future fate will be what it deserves in its later existences.

159. *Do souls have occupations in the spirit life? Do they concern themselves with matters other than their joys or sufferings?*

If souls were concerned only with themselves throughout eternity, that would be selfishness, and God, who condemns selfishness, would not approve in the spirit life what is punishable in the corporeal one. Souls or spirits have occupations in keeping with their degree of advancement while at the same time they seek to learn and improve themselves.[63]

160. *What do the sufferings of the soul consist of after death? Are guilty souls tortured in material flames?*

---

[63] See *The Spirits' Book*, no. 558: Occupations and Missions of Spirits. – Auth.

The church nowadays realizes perfectly well that the fire of hell is mental and not physical; however, it does not define the nature of the sufferings. Spirit communications have brought them before our eyes. Through them, we can determine what these sufferings are, and we can be convinced that even though they are not the result of material fire – which in effect could not burn non-material souls – they are no less horrifying in certain cases. Such sufferings are not uniform and vary infinitely according to the nature and degree of the wrongs committed, and it is nearly always these very wrongs that serve as punishment. It is thus that certain murderers are forced to remain at the place of their crime and to see their victims continuously in front of them; that persons of sensualistic and materialistic tastes retain these same tastes, and the impossibility of physically satisfying them is true torture; that misers believe they are suffering from the cold and the privations they endured while alive because of their miserliness; that other misers remain close to the hoards they buried and experience unending anxiety out of the fear that they might get stolen; in other words, there is not one wrong, one moral imperfection, one evil act that does not have its counterpart and natural consequences in the world of spirits; hence, there is no need for a determined and circumscribed place: everywhere the wicked spirit goes, it carries its own hell with it.

Besides spiritual punishments, there are physical punishments and trials that the not-yet-purified spirit must endure in new incarnations, where it is placed in a position to bear what it made others bear: being humiliated if it had been proud, poverty stricken if it had misused its wealth, made unhappy by its child if it had been a bad child itself, etc. As we have stated, the earth is a place of exile and expiation – *a purgatory* – for spirits of that nature. It will depend on each one not to have to return, seeking to improve itself enough to deserve going to a better world.[64]

161. *Is prayer beneficial for suffering souls?*

Prayer is recommended by all good spirits; moreover, it is asked for by imperfect spirits as a means of relieving their suffering. The soul who is prayed for experiences relief because it is a display of interest, and the unfortunate soul is always relieved when it encounters caring hearts that show compassion for its pain. Also, prayer stimulates repentance and the desire to do what it must to be happy; thus, prayer can shorten its punishment, if, on its part, the suffering soul seconds it through its own goodwill.[65]

162. *What do the pleasures of blissful souls entail? Do such spirits spend eternity in contemplation?*

Justice demands that the reward be proportional to the merit, just as the punishment to the gravity of the wrong; hence, there are infinite degrees in the pleasures of the soul from the moment it enters the path of the good until it attains perfection.

The blissfulness of good spirits entails the knowledge of all things and not having any hatred, jealousy, envy, ambition or any of the other passions that make human beings unhappy. The love that unites them is for them the source of supreme bliss. They do not experience the needs, suffering or anxieties of physical life. A state of unending contemplation would be a senseless and monotonous happiness proper for a selfish spirit, since its existence would be one of unlimited uselessness. Spirit life, on the contrary, is one of

---

[64] See *The Spirits' Book*, no. 237: *Perceptions, Sensations and Sufferings of Spirits*; ibid, Part Four: *Hopes and Consolations; Future Punishments and Rewards; Revue Spirite*, 1858, p. 79: *L'assassin Lemaire*; ibid, 1858, p. 166: *Le suicidé de la Samaritaine*; ibid, 1858, p. 331: *Sensations des Esprits*; ibid, 1859, p. 275: *Le père Crépin*; ibid, 1860, p. 61: *Estelle Régnier*; ibid, 1860, p. 247: *Le suicidé de la rue Quincampoix*; ibid, 1860, p. 316: *Le Châtiment*; ibid, 1860, p. 325: *Entrée d'un coupable dans le monde des Esprits*; ibid, 1860, p. 384: *Châtiment de l'égoïste*; ibid, 1861, p. 53: *Suicide d'un athée*; ibid, 1861, p. 270: *La peine du talion*. – Auth.

[65] See *The Spirits' Book*, no. 664; *Revue Spirite*, 1859, p. 315: *Effects de la prière sur les Esprits souffrants*. – Auth.

ceaseless activity because of the missions that spirits receive from the Supreme Being as his agents in the governance of the universe; missions that are in keeping with their advancement and that they are happy to fulfill since they furnish them with opportunities to make themselves useful and to do the good.[66]

> Comment: We invite the adversaries of Spiritism and those who do not accept reincarnation to provide a more logical solution to the problems discussed above by using a principle other than that of the plurality of existences.

---

[66] See *The Spirits' Book*, no. 558: *Occupations and Missions of Spirits; Revue Spirite*, 1860, p. 321 and 322: *Les purs Esprits; Le séjour des bienheureux;* ibid, 1861, p. 179: *Madame Gourdon.* – Auth.

ALLAN KARDEC

Is the pen name of Hippolyte Léon Denizard Rivail, who was born in Lyon, France on October 3, 1804. He studied at Yverdon (Switzerland) with the famous Johann Heinrich Pestalozzi, becoming his eminent disciple and collaborator. A distinguished linguist, he spoke several languages and his broad education entailed all the branches of human knowledge.

In Paris, he applied himself to spreading the educational system that so greatly influenced the reform of study in France and Germany. He authored books on grammar, arithmetic, upper-level pedagogical studies, and translated English and German works. In his own home, he organized free courses on chemistry, physics, astronomy and comparative anatomy.

But it was as Allan Kardec that he became known worldwide. Guided by high order spirits under the coordination of Spirit of Truth, the Codifier of the Spiritist Doctrine published, successively, The Spirits' Book (1857), The Medium's Book (1861), The Gospel according to Spiritism (1864), Heaven and Hell (1865) and Genesis (1868). Apart from the five-volume Codification he also wrote What is Spiritism? (1859), and in 1890, his friends edited unprinted texts and personal annotations and published Posthumous Works.

In January of 1858, Kardec began publishing the Revue Spirite (Spiritist Review) and in April of the same year he founded the Parisian Society for Spiritist Studies. Both were enterprises which contributed much to the spread of Spiritism and which relied on his guidance until his discarnation on March 31, 1869.